Good Housekeeping

CONFIDENT
COOKING

Good Housekeeping

CONFIDENT
COOKING

The foolproof, step-by-step guide to
mastering essential recipes, from pastry
and soufflés to sauces and roasts

EBURY PRESS
LONDON

First published 1995

1 3 5 7 9 10 8 6 4 2

First published in the United Kingdom in 1995 by
Ebury Press, Random House, 20 Vauxhall Bridge Road, London SW1V 2SA

Random House Australia (Pty) Limited
20 Alfred Street, Milsons Point, Sydney,
New South Wales 2061, Australia

Random House New Zealand Limited
18 Poland Road, Glenfield,
Auckland 10, New Zealand

Random House South Africa (Pty) Limited
PO Box 337, Bergvlei, South Africa

Random House UK Limited Reg. No. 954009

A CIP catalogue record for this book is available from the British Library.

Edited by Helen Southall
Designed and typeset by Behram Kapadia

ISBN 0 09 180781 6

Printed in Italy Officine Grafiche De Agostini - Novara 1995
Bound by Legatoria del Verbano S.p.A.

The publishers would like to thank Le Cordon Bleu Cookery School for permission to reproduce the recipe for Pâte Sucrée on page 44.

CONTENTS

INTRODUCTION

There are some aspects of cookery which never change, such as the need for a sound knowledge of basic techniques. It is these skills that lie at the heart of many of our best-loved recipes, from light and fluffy soufflés to perfect roasts. Yet many of today's cooks feel they have lost, or never acquired, these techniques. *Good Housekeeping Confident Cooking* aims to provide even the most inexperienced cook with the know-how they need to succeed with classic dishes.

Each chapter focuses on a key area, from pastry and sauces, to roasts and baking, and the core technique is illustrated by a basic recipe with step-by-step photographs and clear instructions making it easy to follow. Tips and watchpoints highlight any potential problems and pitfalls. The basic recipe is then followed by a choice of dishes which offer variations and exciting new twists to the original.

Chapter by chapter this book builds into an invaluable cookery reference guide offering expert advice from the renowned kitchens of the Good Housekeeping Institute, as well as providing an impressive selection of delicious recipes. Whether you are entertaining or simply preparing a family meal, you will find all the inspiration and information you need to be confident of success every time.

SAUCES

A good sauce can be the making of a meal, and the classic French sauces have been used for centuries to enhance and complement the foods with which they are served. Despite their reputation, there should be no mystique attached to the making of classic sauces; if you follow the step-by-step instructions on the following pages, success is guaranteed.

Both roux-based and emulsified sauces are included in this chapter. The classic roux-based white sauce is Béchamel; it has many variations and is also used in baked dishes, such as lasagne. Emulsion-based sauces like Hollandaise and Mayonnaise require careful attention because of their tendency to separate, but the technique is easily mastered with practice. The best known sweet sauce is custard, the classic version of which, crème anglaise, is also featured in this chapter. As well as an accompaniment to desserts, it also forms the basis of bavarois and rich, creamy ice creams.

Mayonnaise

With its glorious golden colour and rich flavour, homemade mayonnaise is one of a cook's most useful sauces. It has a reputation for being difficult, but once you've mastered the techniques it will become easier. Overleaf, you'll find recipes to make the most of homemade mayonnaise.

Basic Mayonnaise

MAKES ABOUT 300 ML (½ PINT)

100 CALORIES/15 ML (1 LEVEL TBSP)

NOT SUITABLE FOR FREEZING

2 egg yolks

salt and pepper

pinch of mustard powder

150 ml (¼ pint) olive oil

150 ml (¼ pint) light vegetable oil, such as sunflower oil

about 20 ml (4 tsp) white wine vinegar, cider vinegar or lemon juice

Blender Mayonnaise

Add one whole egg to the basic recipe to cover the blades of the blender or food processor. Blend the yolks, egg and seasoning as in step 1. With the motor on, drizzle the oils down the feed tube. The vinegar should not be added until two-thirds of the oil is incorporated. Adjust the seasoning.

1 Place the egg yolks in a medium bowl with 2.5 ml (½ level tsp) salt, a few 'turns' of freshly ground pepper and the mustard powder. Using a balloon whisk or an electric whisk, beat the egg yolks and seasoning until they have thickened slightly and darkened in colour. Whisk the yolks the moment they are separated. If left uncovered, a crust will form on the surface.

2 Mix the oils in a measuring jug and very slowly drip the oil on to the egg yolks, beating all the time. The mixture should begin to thicken and become smooth and shiny. Keep adding the oil slowly until the mixture has thickened considerably – this usually takes about one-third to half of the oil. Adding oil too quickly will make the mayonnaise curdle and separate.

3 Now whisk in half the vinegar, that is 10 ml (2 tsp). This will thin down the mayonnaise and help to stabilize it. The rest of the oil can now be added more quickly without the risk of curdling.

4 Gradually whisk in the remaining oil, adding it in a slow, steady stream, ensuring that the mayonnaise remains thick and shiny. If the mayonnaise becomes too thick as you add the oil, add 5 ml (1 tsp) vinegar. Continue adding the oil. Finally, whisk in the remaining vinegar and adjust the seasoning.

5 Transfer the mayonnaise to a clean bowl. Press a piece of damp greaseproof paper over the surface to prevent a skin forming. Cover and refrigerate until needed – not more than two weeks. The texture of the finished mayonnaise is much thicker than that of bought, but can be thinned (see Watchpoints). Remove from the refrigerator before using.

Watchpoints

These tips will help you avoid the most common pitfalls:

Mayonnaise curdles (the eggs and oil separate)

• Vigorously whisk or beat.

• If this fails, add about 15 ml (1 tbsp) hot water to the mayonnaise and beat well – the warmth should help to bring the mayonnaise together again.

• If the mayonnaise is badly curdled (almost liquid), start again with fresh egg yolks and oil and when well thickened, add the curdled mixture slowly, as if it were oil alone – this will make a slightly thicker mayonnaise.

Mayonnaise separates when used straight from the refrigerator

• Stirred when very cold, it may separate. Remove from the refrigerator and leave for 1 hour before using.

Mayonnaise too thick

• Mix in a little warm water, single cream or lemon juice. Add with care as the mayonnaise quickly thins.

Raw eggs

The young, the elderly, pregnant women and people with immune-deficiency diseases should not eat raw eggs, due to the possible risk of salmonella. Use bottled mayonnaise, in which the eggs have been pasteurized.

Prawn Cocktail (page 13)

Mustardy Potato Salad

SERVES 4

375 CALORIES/SERVING

700 g (1½ lb) very small potatoes, scrubbed

salt and pepper

parsley sprigs, to garnish

For the dressing

225 ml (8 fl oz) fromage frais

75 ml (5 tbsp) Basic Mayonnaise (see page 10)

30 ml (2 level tbsp) wholegrain mustard

10 ml (2 level tsp) Dijon mustard

1 Cook the potatoes in their skins in boiling salted water for about 10 minutes or until tender. Meanwhile, mix together the ingredients for the dressing and season with salt and pepper.
2 When the potatoes are cooked, drain them well and add them to the dressing, tossing well so they are completely coated in the dressing. Leave to cool before serving, garnished with parsley.

Cook's tip
French smooth-skinned potato varieties, such as La Ratte, Cornichon or Belle de Fontenay, make excellent potato salads. Alternatively, the English Pink Fir Apple variety is equally delicious and well worth looking for.

Glazed Vegetable Pastries

To make Garlic Mayonnaise, add two small crushed cloves of garlic to the Basic Mayonnaise recipe (see page 10). The pastries in step 1 can be made a day ahead and kept in an airtight container. Cook the vegetables the day before and store in the refrigerator. Make the mayonnaise and refrigerate. To complete, plunge the vegetables in boiling water for 1 minute to warm through, then continue assembling as in step 3.

SERVES 6

250 CALORIES/SERVING

filo pastry

25 g (1 oz) butter, melted

350 g (12 oz) mixed baby vegetables, such as corn, mangetouts and carrots

salt and pepper

about 60 ml (4 level tbsp) Garlic Mayonnaise

15 ml (1 level tbsp) chopped fresh mixed herbs

50 g (2 oz) soft, fresh goat's cheese

single cream

1 Cut the filo pastry into six squares measuring about 10 cm (4 inches) each. Place, singly, on buttered, upturned Yorkshire pudding tins and brush the pastry with butter. Bake in the oven at 190°C (375°F) mark 5 for 7–8 minutes or until golden. Gently lift the pastry off the upturned tins.
2 Cook the vegetables in boiling salted water until just tender. Drain well. Beat together the next three ingredients. Add enough single cream to give a coating consistency.
3 Place the vegetables in the pastry cases, and spoon over the mayonnaise mixture. Glaze under a hot grill for 1 minute and serve.

Coronation Chicken

Originally created by the Cordon Bleu Cookery School for the Queen's coronation, this is a very popular chicken dish, particulary for including in a buffet spread. This version includes saffron and a dash of cream. It's easier to make up the curry mixture in large quantities, so this recipe makes double the quantity you need. Use half the sauce mixture for the Coronation Chicken and freeze the rest of the sauce for another day.

SERVES 4 AS A MAIN MEAL OR 6 AS PART OF A BUFFET

465 CALORIES/SERVING FOR 6

1.6–1.8 kg (3½–4 lb) oven-ready chicken
slices of carrot and onion, I bay leaf and peppercorns for flavouring
salt and pepper
50 g (2 oz) butter
225 g (8 oz) onion, peeled and chopped
8 no-soak dried apricots
large pinch of saffron strands
grated rind of 2 lemons
60 ml (4 tbsp) runny honey
75 ml (5 level tbsp) curry paste
450 ml (¾ pint) dry white wine
½ quantity Basic Mayonnaise, i.e. I egg yolk, 150 ml (¼ pint) mixed oils, etc. (see page 10)
45 ml (3 level tbsp) double cream
fresh herbs, to garnish

1 Place the chicken in a large saucepan. Add the flavouring ingredients with a large pinch of salt. Bring to the boil, cover and simmer for 1–1¼ hours or until the chicken is thoroughly cooked. Cool in the liquid.
2 Cut the chicken into bite-sized pieces, discarding skin and bone. Cover and refrigerate until required.
3 Melt the butter in a saucepan and sauté the onion until softened. Add the apricots, saffron, lemon rind, honey, curry paste and white wine. Simmer, uncovered, for 30–40 minutes or until the curry mixture is the consistency of thin chutney. Leave to cool, then blend in a food processor and pass through a sieve.
4 Stir half of the curry mixture into the mayonnaise (freeze the remainder). Mix in the double cream and season with salt and pepper.
5 Fold the chicken through the sauce (this can be done the day before, then covered and refrigerated). Serve garnished with sprigs of fresh herbs.

Freezer notes for Coronation Chicken
To freeze: Cool, pack and freeze the cooked chicken and the completed curry sauce separately.
To use: Thaw both chicken and sauce overnight at cool room temperature. Whisk the sauce. Complete as in the recipe.

Prawn Cocktails

SERVES 4

200 CALORIES/SERVING

60 ml (4 tbsp) Basic Mayonnaise (see page 10)
60 ml (4 tbsp) single cream
10 ml (2 level tsp) tomato purée
10 ml (2 tsp) lemon juice
dash of Worcestershire sauce
dash of dry sherry
salt and pepper
225 g (8 oz) cooked peeled prawns
few lettuce leaves, shredded
lemon slices, to garnish

1 In a small bowl, mix together the mayonnaise, cream, tomato purée, lemon juice, Worcestershire sauce and sherry. Season with salt and pepper. Add the prawns and stir well to coat.
2 Place the shredded lettuce in four glasses and top with the prawn mixture.
3 Garnish each prawn cocktail with lemon slices. Serve with thinly sliced brown bread.

Béchamel Sauce

This classic roux-based sauce is the basis of many other savoury sauces (see below). Use for fish, poultry, egg and vegetable dishes. The consistency of the sauce can be changed by increasing the proportions of fat and flour to milk. A thicker Béchamel is used for coating and binding foods.

MAKES 300 ML (½ PINT)

180 CALORIES/150 ML (¼ PINT)

300 ml (½ pint) milk
1 slice of onion
1 bay leaf
6 peppercorns
1 blade of mace
15 g (½ oz) butter or margarine
15 g (½ oz) white plain flour
salt and pepper
freshly grated nutmeg

VARIATIONS

Thick Béchamel Sauce
Increase the butter and flour to 25 g (1 oz) each.

Simple White Sauce
Omit the flavouring ingredients and the infusing stage; simply stir cold milk into the roux.

Cheese (Mornay) Sauce
Off the heat, stir in 50 g (2 oz) finely grated mature Cheddar or Gruyère cheese and a large pinch of mustard powder.

Parsley Sauce
Add about 30 ml (2 level tbsp) chopped fresh parsley.

Onion (Soubise) Sauce
Finely dice 1 onion, then sauté in a little butter for 10–15 minutes until softened. Stir into the Béchamel. Purée in a blender or food processor, if preferred.

Mushroom Sauce
Thinly slice 75 g (3 oz) mushrooms and sweat them gently in a little butter until tender. Stir into the Béchamel.

1 Pour the milk into a saucepan. Add the onion, bay leaf, peppercorns and mace. Bring to scalding point, then remove from the heat, cover, and leave to infuse for 10–30 minutes. Strain.

2 To make the roux, melt the butter in a saucepan. Stir in the flour and cook, stirring, for 1 minute.

3 Remove from the heat and gradually pour on the warm milk, whisking constantly. Season lightly with salt, pepper and nutmeg.

4 Return to the heat and bring to the boil, whisking constantly until the sauce thickens and is smooth. Simmer for 2–3 minutes.

Freezer notes
To freeze: Pack and freeze.
To use: Thaw at cool room temperature, then whisk. Reheat gently in a small saucepan, whisking constantly.

Watchpoints
• It is important to remove the pan from the heat in step 3, and to add the milk to the roux very gradually, whisking well between each addition.
• If lumps form, they can usually be removed by vigorous whisking. If not, work the sauce through a sieve, or put it in a blender and blend until smooth, then return to the saucepan to reheat gently.

Cook's tip
To prevent a skin forming on the sauce while it cools, cover the surface with a damp piece of greaseproof paper. Alternatively, dot the surface with tiny pieces of butter, which will melt and form a thin coating. Beat the butter into the sauce before using.

RIGHT: *Boiled Bacon with Parsley Sauce (page 16)*

Boiled Bacon with Parsley Sauce

SERVES 6–8

515–385 CALORIES/SERVING

1.4 kg (3 lb) gammon, collar or forehock bacon joint
2 onions, peeled and quartered
2 carrots, peeled and quartered
2 celery sticks, chopped
1 bay leaf
4 black peppercorns
parsley sprigs, to garnish
300 ml (½ pint) Parsley Sauce (see page 14), to serve

1 Weigh the joint and calculate the cooking time, allowing 20 minutes per 450 g (1 lb) plus 20 minutes.
2 To remove the salt, place the joint in a large saucepan and cover with cold water. Bring slowly to the boil, then remove from the heat and strain off the water.
3 Add the vegetables, bay leaf and peppercorns to the joint in the saucepan. Cover with fresh cold water and bring slowly to the boil. Skim the surface with a slotted spoon. Cover and simmer gently for the calculated cooking time.
4 Remove the bacon from the pan. Ease off the rind and remove any excess fat. Carve into slices and serve hot, garnished with parsley and accompanied by the parsley sauce.

Vegetable Lasagne

SERVES 6

365 CALORIES/SERVING

30 ml (2 tbsp) olive oil
1 garlic clove, crushed
1 carrot, peeled and chopped
1 large onion, peeled and sliced
1 red pepper, deseeded and chopped
15 ml (1 level tbsp) mild paprika
10 ml (2 level tsp) dried oregano or marjoram
1 large aubergine, cut into chunks
225 g (8 oz) button mushrooms, wiped and sliced
2 large courgettes, sliced
two 400 g (14 oz) cans chopped tomatoes
30 ml (2 level tbsp) tomato purée
2 bay leaves
salt and pepper
about 350 g (12 oz) fresh lasagne or 225 g (8 oz) oven-ready dried lasagne
900 ml (1½ pints) Béchamel Sauce (see page 14)
45 ml (3 level tbsp) freshly grated Parmesan or Cheddar cheese (optional)

1 Heat the oil in a large saucepan. Add the garlic, carrot, onion and red pepper, and fry for 1–2 minutes or until beginning to soften. Add the paprika, herbs and aubergine, and fry for 1–2 minutes.

2 Add the remaining vegetables to the pan with the tomatoes, tomato purée and bay leaves. Season with salt and pepper. Bring to the boil, then reduce the heat, cover and simmer for about 30 minutes.

3 Spread about one third of the tomato sauce in the base of a shallow 2.8 litre (5 pint) ovenproof dish. Cover with a layer of lasagne and top with a layer of Béchamel Sauce. Repeat the layers twice more, ending with a layer of Béchamel Sauce.

4 Sprinkle with the cheese, if using, and bake in the oven at 190°C (375°F) mark 5 for 45–50 minutes or until the lasagne is piping hot and well browned. Leave to stand for 5 minutes before serving with a crisp salad.

Moussaka

SERVES 6

490 CALORIES/SERVING

oil
175 g (6 oz) onion, peeled and chopped
450 g (1 lb) lean minced beef or lamb
400 g (14 oz) can chopped tomatoes
1.25 ml (¼ level tsp) ground cinnamon
5 ml (1 level tsp) dried oregano
salt and pepper
900 g (2 lb) aubergines, sliced
30 ml (2 level tbsp) fresh breadcrumbs
For the sauce
75 g (3 oz) butter
75 g (3 oz) white plain flour
568 ml (1 pint) warm milk
25 g (1 oz) Parmesan cheese, freshly grated
1 egg yolk
salt and pepper

1 Heat 30 ml (2 tbsp) oil in a frying pan and fry the onion for about 5 minutes or until soft. Stir in the meat and fry until it changes colour. Add the tomatoes, cinnamon and oregano, and season with salt and pepper.

Cover and cook for 20 minutes or until all liquid has evaporated.

2 Brush the aubergine slices with oil and grill until golden on both sides. Drain on absorbent kitchen paper.

3 For the sauce, follow steps 2–4 of Béchamel Sauce (see page 14), but do not season the sauce at the end of step 4. Remove from the heat, cool slightly, then beat in half the cheese and the egg yolk. Season with salt and pepper.

4 Season the aubergine slices with salt and pepper and place in a 2.8 litre (5 pint) shallow, ovenproof dish. Spread the meat mixture on top and cover with the sauce. Sprinkle over the remaining cheese and the breadcrumbs.

5 Cook in the oven at 180°C (350°F) mark 4 for about 1 hour or until golden.

Hollandaise Sauce

Hollandaise is one of the classic 'emulsified' sauces, based on an emulsion of butter and egg yolks. Traditionally served with asparagus, it is an excellent accompaniment to many vegetables.

SERVES 4

215 CALORIES/SERVING

NOT SUITABLE FOR FREEZING

45 ml (3 tbsp) white wine vinegar

6 peppercorns

1 small bay leaf

1 blade of mace

75–125 g (3–4 oz) butter, at room temperature

2 egg yolks

salt

1 Put the vinegar, peppercorns, bay leaf and mace in a small saucepan and boil rapidly until reduced to only 10 ml (2 tsp). Remove from the heat and strain. Soften the butter until it is creamy.

2 Put the egg yolks in a small heatproof bowl. Add a pinch of salt and the flavoured vinegar, and whisk until thoroughly combined.

3 Set the bowl over a saucepan of gently simmering water over a low heat and whisk for about 3 minutes or until the mixture is thick enough to leave a trail when the whisk is lifted.

4 Gradually add the butter, a little at a time, whisking constantly. When 75 g (3 oz) has been added, season lightly with salt. Taste the sauce and, if it is still too sharp, add more butter.

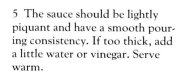

5 The sauce should be lightly piquant and have a smooth pouring consistency. If too thick, add a little water or vinegar. Serve warm.

Watchpoints
• Hollandaise should be cooked very slowly and gently. The water in the saucepan beneath the bowl should be barely simmering; a fierce heat will produce a granular texture and, if overcooked, the eggs will scramble.
• If the sauce begins to curdle, remove it from the heat, add an ice cube and whisk well. This should bring the emulsion back together.

Cook's tip
If not serving the Hollandaise immediately, remove the sauce from the heat and keep it warm over a saucepan of warm (not hot) water.

RIGHT: *Asparagus with Coriander Hollandaise (page 20)*

Asparagus with Coriander Hollandaise

SERVES 4

295 CALORIES/SERVING

450 g (1 lb) asparagus
salt
15 ml (1 tbsp) lemon juice
blanched lemon rind strips and fresh chervil sprigs, to garnish
For the sauce
125 g (4 oz) unsalted butter, diced
25 ml (1½ level tbsp) coriander seeds, crushed and lightly toasted
25 ml (1½ tbsp) lemon juice
10 ml (2 tsp) white wine vinegar
2 egg yolks
pinch of sugar
pinch of salt

1 To make the sauce, melt the butter in a saucepan, add the coriander seeds, and warm gently until the butter just begins to bubble. Remove from the heat, cover and leave to infuse for 20 minutes.

2 Meanwhile, scrape the asparagus stalks and remove the woody ends. Arrange the asparagus, tips together, in two equal bundles and tie them with string. Stand the bundles upright in a saucepan of boiling salted water, to which the lemon juice has been added, with the tips out of the water.

3 Cover with a lid or dome of foil and cook gently for about 10 minutes or until tender, depending on the size of the spears.

4 For the sauce, put the lemon juice and vinegar in a saucepan and bring to the boil. Gently reheat the coriander butter until just beginning to foam.

5 Put the egg yolks, sugar and salt in a blender and blend briefly, then, with the motor running, slowly pour in the lemon juice and vinegar mixture. When it has all been absorbed, slowly pour in the coriander butter, with the motor still running.

6 Drain the asparagus well and arrange on warmed serving plates. Spoon the coriander hollandaise over the asparagus. Garnish with strips of lemon rind and sprigs of chervil.

Baked Salmon Steaks with Hollandaise Sauce

SERVES 8

540 CALORIES/SERVING

8 salmon steaks, about 175 g (6 oz) each
50 g (2 oz) butter
salt and pepper
lemon juice, to taste
fresh tarragon sprigs, to garnish
For the sauce
45 ml (3 tbsp) wine or tarragon vinegar
3 egg yolks
350 g (12 oz) unsalted butter, softened
salt and white pepper

1 Line two baking sheets with buttered foil. Place the salmon on the foil, dot each steak with butter and season with salt, pepper and lemon juice.

2 Wrap loosely and bake in the oven at 180°C (350°F) mark 4 for 20–30 minutes, depending on the thickness of the fish.

3 Meanwhile, to make the sauce, put the vinegar and 15–30 ml (1–2 tbsp) water in a saucepan. Boil gently until reduced by half, then cool.

4 Put the egg yolks and reduced vinegar liquid in a double saucepan or heatproof bowl over a pan of gently simmering water, and whisk until thick and fluffy.

5 Gradually add the butter, a tiny piece at a time, whisking briskly after each addition until the piece has been absorbed. The final sauce should be the consistency of mayonnaise. Taste and season with salt and white pepper. If the sauce is too sharp, add a little more butter.
6 Serve the salmon garnished with tarragon and accompanied by the Hollandaise sauce and seasonal vegetables.

Lemon Sole with Mousseline Sauce

Mousseline sauce is a richer version of Hollandaise, with whipped cream added to the sauce just before serving.

SERVES 6

260 CALORIES/SERVING

2 egg yolks	
10 ml (2 tsp) lemon juice	
salt and pepper	
50 g (2 oz) unsalted butter, softened	
12 single lemon sole fillets	
melted butter, for brushing	
50 ml (2 fl oz) whipping cream	

1 To make the mousseline sauce, place the egg yolks in a small heatproof bowl. Add 5 ml (1 tsp) of the lemon juice, and season with salt and pepper. Add a knob of the softened unsalted butter. Set the bowl over a saucepan of gently simmering water and whisk well until the mixture is quite thick.
2 Remove the bowl from the heat and whisk in the rest of the softened butter, a small piece at a time. Add the remaining lemon juice. Return the bowl to the saucepan over a low heat to keep the sauce warm.
3 Brush the sole fillets with melted butter and grill for 2–3 minutes on each side.
4 Lightly whip the cream and fold into the sauce. Serve the grilled sole fillets immediately, with the mousseline sauce spooned over.

Béarnaise Sauce

Béarnaise is an enriched version of Hollandaise sauce, with a more pungent flavour. It is traditionally served as an accompaniment to grilled meats.

SERVES 4

480 CALORIES/SERVING

I shallot, peeled and finely chopped	
20 ml (4 level tsp) chopped fresh tarragon	
10 ml (2 level tsp) chopped fresh chervil	
75 ml (3 fl oz) dry white wine	
75 ml (3 fl oz) tarragon vinegar	
pinch of crushed white peppercorns	
pinch of salt	
3 egg yolks	
225 g (8 oz) butter, melted	
freshly ground pepper	

1 Put the shallot, 5 ml (1 level tsp) of the tarragon, 2.5 ml (½ level tsp) of the chervil, the white wine and tarragon vinegar in a saucepan. Add the peppercorns and salt, and boil until reduced by two thirds. Allow to cool.
2 Transfer the mixture to a small heatproof bowl set over a saucepan of gently simmering water. Add the egg yolks and whisk over a gentle heat for about 3 minutes to form an emulsion.
3 Gradually add the tepid melted butter, whisking well after each addition. Strain the sauce through a muslin-lined sieve or a fine strainer.
4 Taste and adjust the seasoning, and stir in the remaining tarragon and chervil. Serve warm.

Crème Anglaise

Crème Anglaise is a lightly thickened 'real' custard, ideal for special occasions when you want a sweet sauce to accompany desserts. It's also the base for rich, creamy bavarois (set custard) and wonderful ice creams.

SERVES 4

115 CALORIES/SERVING

½ vanilla pod

300 ml (½ pint) milk

3 egg yolks

20 ml (4 level tsp) caster sugar

VARIATIONS

Orange, Lemon or Mint Custard

Omit the vanilla pod. Add the pared rind of ½ orange or ½ lemon or a handful of washed mint to the milk and bring to the boil. Complete as above, using 20 ml (4 level tsp) sugar and straining the milk on to the egg yolks.

Chocolate Crème Anglaise

Omit the vanilla pod. Break up 50 g (2 oz) plain chocolate and bring slowly to the boil with the milk, whisking until smooth. Complete as above, using 15 ml (1 level tbsp) sugar only.

Nutmeg and Sherry Custard

Omit the vanilla pod. Prepare the custard as above, adding a dash of grated nutmeg and 15–30 ml (1–2 tbsp) sherry at the end.

Extra Creamy Crème Anglaise

Replace half or all the milk with single cream, or half single and half double cream.

1 Split open the vanilla pod and scrape out the seeds into a medium, heavy-based saucepan. Add the pod and the milk. Bring slowly to the boil, then remove from the heat, cover and leave to infuse for 30 minutes. Remove the vanilla pod.

2 Place the egg yolks and sugar in a medium bowl. Using a balloon whisk, electric whisk or wooden spoon, beat the yolks and sugar until they lighten in colour and thicken slightly.

3 Pour the infused milk on to the mixture, whisking or stirring until evenly mixed. Rinse out the saucepan, then return the mixture to the pan. Have ready a cold bowl with a sieve over the top.

4 Place the saucepan over a low to moderate heat, and stir the custard all the time until it thickens slightly and begins to coat the back of the spoon (about 10 minutes). Do not boil the custard or it will curdle. Watch the froth on the custard – when it begins to disappear, the custard is starting to thicken.

5 Immediately strain the custard into the cold bowl to stop it cooking. Whisk to reduce the temperature. To serve warm, pour into a jug. To serve cold, place damp greaseproof paper on the surface of the hot custard to prevent a skin forming. Cool, then chill.

Freezer notes

To freeze: Pack and freeze.
To use: Thaw at cool room temperature for 6 hours, then whisk. Reheat without boiling, whisking occasionally. All the variations, except the Nutmeg and Sherry Custard, will also freeze well.

Watchpoints

• It is important to rinse out the saucepan in step 3, before heating the mixture, to avoid the custard burning on to the base of the pan.

• If the custard begins to separate and look like runny scrambled eggs, it is curdling. To rescue it, strain it immediately into a cold bowl, add a few ice cubes and whisk vigorously to reduce the temperature – it should smooth out again quite quickly.

Cook's Tips

• Crème Anglaise should be silky smooth with no sign of curdling, so it must never boil. It can be made in a double saucepan, but this is very slow. If you're careful using a saucepan, you'll have perfect custard every time. If you are nervous of curdling the custard, beat 5 ml (1 level tsp) cornflour with the yolks in step 2. This helps thicken the custard, but taste it after cooking to ensure that all traces of cornflour have disappeared. If necessary, stir over a gentle heat for a little longer, but do not boil.

• For convenience, a few drops of vanilla essence can replace the vanilla pod. Add to the milk at the beginning of step 3.

Nutmeg and Sherry Custard served as a luxurious accompaniment to Mille Feuilles

Vanilla Ice Cream

For a richer ice cream, prepare the Crème Anglaise with half single cream and half milk.

SERVES 6

335 CALORIES/SERVING

300 ml (½ pint) milk
½ vanilla pod
3 egg yolks
75 g (3 oz) caster sugar
284 ml (10 fl oz) carton double cream
pared, blanched lemon rind, to decorate (optional)

1 Using the milk, vanilla pod, egg yolks and sugar, prepare the custard as in steps 1–4 of Crème Anglaise (page 22). Remove from the heat, strain and cool.
2 Whip the cream until it just begins to hold its shape, and stir gently into the custard.
3 Pour into a shallow freezer container and freeze for 3–4 hours or until mushy.
4 Take the mushy ice cream out of the freezer and lightly beat with a fork or balloon whisk to break down the ice crystals.
5 Return the ice cream to the freezer and freeze for about 3 hours or until firm.
6 Before serving, allow the ice cream to soften in the refrigerator for 1–1½ hours. Decorate with pared, blanched lemon rind if wished.

VARIATIONS

Praline
Prepare the ice cream as above to the end of step 3, using 25 g (1 oz) sugar only. While the mixture is in the freezer, prepare the praline. Place 50 g (2 oz) almonds (with skins) and 50 g (2 oz) caster sugar in a small frying pan. Heat gently until the sugar melts and caramelizes – do not stir, just prod the sugar occasionally with a wooden spoon to help it brown evenly. Pour the caramelized nuts on to an oiled baking sheet, and leave to cool and set. Once cold, grind in a food processor or through a nut mouli to a fine powder. Beat the ice cream as in step 4, then stir in the praline. Freeze as above.

Lemon
Using 3 egg yolks, 300 ml (½ pint) milk, 150 g (5 oz) caster sugar and the pared rind of 3 lemons, prepare a lemon custard as in the Crème Anglaise variation on page 22. Cool, then stir in 75 ml (5 tbsp) strained lemon juice and 284 ml (10 fl oz) whipped double cream. Complete and freeze as in steps 3–6 of Vanilla Ice Cream.

Snow Eggs

In this elegant dessert, poached meringues float in a smooth, coffee-flavoured Crème Anglaise.

SERVES 6

200 CALORIES/SERVING

10 ml (2 tsp) coffee beans
3 eggs, separated
75 g (3 oz) caster sugar
450 ml (¾ pint) milk
50 g (2 oz) milk chocolate
30 ml (2 tbsp) whisky
blackberries, to decorate (optional)

1 Toast the coffee beans under the grill for a few minutes.
2 To make the meringue, whisk the egg whites until stiff but not dry. Add half the sugar and continue whisking until the mixture is firm and shiny.
3 Put the milk in a large, deep frying pan. Bring to the boil, then reduce the heat to a gentle simmer. Drop five or six spoonfuls of the meringue mixture into the milk and poach for about 5 minutes, turning once. Remove with a slotted spoon and drain on absorbent kitchen paper. Repeat until all the mixture is used; there should be about 18 meringues.
4 Whisk the egg yolks and remaining sugar into the poaching milk, then add the coffee beans. Stir over a very gentle heat for 10–12 minutes or until slightly thickened, making sure it does not boil. Strain the coffee custard into a serving dish and arrange the meringues on top.
5 Melt the chocolate with 15 ml (1 tbsp) water in a heatproof bowl over a saucepan of hot water until smooth, then stir in the whisky. Drizzle over the meringues. Chill for 15–20 minutes before serving, decorated with blackberries if wished.

Strawberry and Orange Bavarois

A bavarois is a lightly set, flavoured custard. In this recipe, the custard is flavoured with a strawberry purée, and the centre of the bavarois is filled with a bright red fruit sauce.

SERVES 6

270 CALORIES/SERVING

568 ml (1 pint) milk
pared rind and juice of 1 orange
6 egg yolks
75 g (3 oz) caster sugar
450 g (1 lb) ripe strawberries
142 ml (5 fl oz) carton double cream
oil for greasing
20 ml (4 level tsp) powdered gelatine
sprigs of redcurrants and mint leaves, to decorate
For the fruit sauce
350 g (12 oz) raspberries
45 ml (3 level tbsp) icing sugar
225 g (8 oz) small ripe strawberries, halved
15–30 ml (1–2 tbsp) Cointreau (optional)

1 First make the bavarois. Prepare an orange-flavoured custard as in the Crème Anglaise variation on page 22, using the milk, pared orange rind, egg yolks and caster sugar. Remove from the heat and leave to cool.

2 Purée the strawberries in a food processor, then push them gently through a nylon sieve, taking care not to rub the pips through; there should be about 400 ml (14 fl oz) purée. Lightly whip the cream until it just begins to hold its shape. Lightly oil a 1.3–1.4 litre (2¼–2½ pint) ring mould. Turn the mould upside down on a piece of absorbent kitchen paper to allow any excess oil to drain off.

3 Place 60 ml (4 tbsp) orange juice and 30 ml (2 tbsp) water in a small heatproof bowl. Sprinkle over the gelatine and leave to soak for about 10 minutes or until sponge-like in texture. Dissolve by standing the bowl in a saucepan of simmering water until the gelatine clears and liquefies.

4 Stir the dissolved gelatine into the custard. Mix well, then stir in the strawberry purée. Stand the bowl in another, larger bowl full of cold water and ice cubes, and stir frequently until the custard begins to thicken and set to the consistency of lightly whipped cream (about 20 minutes).

5 Immediately remove the bowl from the ice and stir in the cream. Pour the mixture into the prepared mould and refrigerate for about 2 hours or until set.

6 Meanwhile, prepare the fruit sauce. Purée 225 g (8 oz) raspberries with the icing sugar in a food processor, then rub through a nylon sieve. Stir in the halved strawberries and the remaining raspberries with the Cointreau, if using. Cover and chill.

7 To serve the bavarois, invert the mould on to an edged serving plate. Shake gently to release the vacuum and lift off the mould. Fill the centre of the bavarois with some of the fruit sauce and decorate with sprigs of redcurrants and mint leaves. Serve the remaining fruit sauce separately.

PASTRY

Pastry making is a basic culinary skill and one on which countless sweet and savoury dishes depend. The secrets to success lie in light handling and accurate measuring of ingredients, and in carefully following instructions. This chapter begins with simple shortcrust pastry, the basis of so many dishes, from savoury flans and quiches to fruit pies and tarts, and ends with rich, crisp pâte sucrée, the pastry traditionally used for sweet French pâtisserie. Puff pastry recipes, such as sausage rolls and gougère, are also included, as is a selection of old-fashioned, deep-crust pies made with a special enriched shortcrust pastry. All the basic pastry recipes are given; once you have mastered the techniques you can vary the recipes as you please.

Shortcrust Pastry

The most versatile of pastries, shortcrust should be slightly crumbly with a deliciously rich, buttery flavour. It can be made and refrigerated up to 12 hours in advance and it also freezes well – just as it is or shaped into flan cases.

Golden Onion Tart

SERVES 6

530 CALORIES/SERVING

For the pastry

125 g (4 oz) butter

white plain flour

pinch of salt

For the filling

50 g (2 oz) butter

700 g (1½ lb) onions, peeled and sliced

2 whole eggs and 1 egg yolk

142 ml (5 fl oz) carton single cream

150 ml (¼ pint) milk

pinch of freshly grated nutmeg

salt and pepper

30 ml (2 level tbsp) freshly grated Parmesan cheese

125 g (4 oz) mature Cheddar cheese, grated

PASTRY VARIATIONS

Herb Pastry
Add 30 ml (2 level tbsp) chopped fresh mixed herbs to the flour.

Olive Pastry
Mix 25 g (1 oz) finely chopped black olives into the pastry before adding the water.

1 Leave the butter at room temperature for about 30 minutes to soften very slightly. Sift 175 g (6 oz) flour and the salt into a large mixing bowl. Cut the butter into about eight pieces. Using a round-bladed knife, cut the butter into the flour until only small pieces remain. Continue by rubbing the fat and flour between your fingertips until the mixture resembles fine breadcrumbs.

2 Sprinkle 30–45 ml (2–3 tbsp) water on the mixture and cut it through with the knife until evenly mixed. Then, using only one hand, gradually and lightly knead the dough. If very dry, sprinkle a little more water over. If sticky, knead in a little flour. Wrap in greaseproof paper or foil and chill for 30 minutes.
  Lightly flour the work surface and a rolling pin. Knead the dough into an even, round shape, and roll it out. For a neat circle, give three or four rolls, then turn the dough clockwise through about 45°. Roll and turn until you have a 29–30 cm (11½–12 inch) round.

3 Fold the pastry loosely over the rolling pin. Lift the pastry over a 3 cm (1¼ inch) deep, 23 cm (9 inch) base-measurement, loose-based, fluted flan tin. Ease the pastry down into the corners without stretching it. Press it lightly into the tin flutes and roll off excess pastry to neaten the top edges. Prick the base of the flan case with a fork and stand the tin on a baking sheet. Chill for about 30 minutes.

4 Line the flan case with greaseproof paper and baking beans. Bake blind in the oven at 200°C (400°F) mark 6 for 15 minutes. Remove the paper and beans, prick the pastry again and return to the oven for 10–15 minutes or until lightly browned and well dried out. (This step is essential to avoid a soggy pastry base.)

Freezer notes
To freeze: Pack and freeze the baked pastry case only.
To use: Thaw for 2 hours, then complete as in the recipe.

5 Meanwhile, for the filling, melt the butter in a sauté pan and add the onions. Cover and cook over moderate heat for 20–25 minutes or until soft and golden brown, stirring once or twice.

6 Whisk together the eggs, egg yolk, cream, milk and nutmeg, and season with salt and pepper. Add all the Parmesan and three-quarters of the Cheddar cheese. Spoon the onions into the flan case. Pour the egg mixture over and sprinkle with the remaining Cheddar. Bake in the oven at 180°C (350°F) mark 4 for 35–40 minutes or until just set. Cool for about 15 minutes before serving warm.

Watchpoints

• Equipment and fingers should be cool. Run hot hands under the cold tap and dry them well before you start.
• You can prepare the pastry in the food processor, but don't overwork it. Process the butter, flour and salt until the mixture resembles fine breadcrumbs, then add the water until just blended. Knead lightly on the work surface.
• Rub the butter in until evenly mixed but not sticky. If over-rubbed, the dough will be difficult to handle.
• Always add at least the minimum amount of water suggested. The dough may at first seem sticky but will dry out as it cooks. If insufficient liquid is added, the pastry will crumble and fall apart; too much liquid and the pastry will be tough.
• Treat the pastry gently; if you overknead the dough, it will become tough and hard.
• Always roll the pastry away from you. If you try to lean over the dough and roll it from side to side, it will stretch unevenly, causing it to shrink when cooked.
• If you're in a hurry, once the tin is lined the pastry can be chilled for 10 minutes in the freezer.

The Ultimate Cheese Tart

SERVES 6

590 CALORIES/SERVING

75 g (3 oz) butter

white plain flour

pinch of ground paprika

salt and pepper

75 g (3 oz) mature Cheddar cheese, grated

3 eggs, separated

284 ml (10 fl oz) carton single cream

10 ml (2 level tsp) Dijon mustard

150 g (5 oz) Gruyère cheese, grated

75 g (3 oz) feta cheese, crumbled

125 g (4 oz) Brie

pinenuts

tomatoes and fresh herbs, to garnish

1 First prepare the cheese pastry. Rub the butter into 175 g (6 oz) flour, paprika and salt as in step 1 of Golden Onion Tart (see page 28). Stir in the Cheddar cheese and bind to a dough with about 45 ml (3 tbsp) water. Wrap and chill for 30 minutes.

2 Roll out the pastry, line the tin, chill and bake as in steps 2, 3 and 4 of Golden Onion Tart.

3 Whisk together the egg yolks, cream and mustard, and season with salt and pepper. Stir in the Gruyère and feta cheeses. Cut the rind off the Brie and divide the cheese roughly into 1 cm (½ inch) cubes. Stir into the cream mixture.

4 Whisk the egg whites until stiff but not dry and fold into the cream mixture. Gently pour into the pastry case. Sprinkle a few pinenuts over.

5 Bake in the oven at 180°C (350°F) mark 4 for 35–40 minutes or until just set. Cool for about 15 minutes before serving warm, garnished with tomatoes and fresh herbs.

The Ultimate Cheese Tart

Summer Vegetable Flan

Use any selection of summer vegetables for this flan. Blanch or sauté them first, and keep the total amount to about 700 g (1½ lb).

SERVES 6

520 CALORIES/SERVING

50 g (2 oz) walnut pieces

white plain flour

salt and pepper

butter

1 garlic clove, thinly sliced

175 g (6 oz) courgettes, thinly sliced

175 g (6 oz) asparagus

175 g (6 oz) baby carrots, scrubbed

50 g (2 oz) peas

125 g (4 oz) fresh tomatoes

50 g (2 oz) sundried tomatoes

142 ml (5 fl oz) carton single cream

125 g (4 oz) full-fat soft cheese

2 whole eggs and 1 egg yolk

30 ml (2 level tbsp) chopped fresh mixed herbs

40 g (1½ oz) mature Cheddar cheese, grated

chives and fresh herbs, to garnish

1 First prepare the nut pastry. Grill the walnut pieces until golden, cool, then grind to a powder using a blender or nut mouli. Mix with 175 g (6 oz) flour and a pinch of salt, and rub in 75 g (3 oz) butter as in step 1 of Golden Onion Tart (see page 28). Bind to a dough with about 45 ml (3 tbsp) water. Wrap and chill for 30 minutes.

2 Roll out the pastry, line the tin, chill and bake as in steps 2, 3 and 4 of Golden Onion Tart.

3 Meanwhile, sauté the garlic and courgettes together in 25 g (1 oz) butter until golden.

4 Scrape the asparagus stalks and remove the woody stems. Blanch with the carrots and peas in boiling salted water for 1–2 minutes. Drain. Cut the fresh and sundried tomatoes into quarters. Gradually whisk the cream into the soft cheese. Add the eggs, egg yolk and herbs, and season with salt and pepper. Mix well.

5 Pile all the vegetables into the flan case and pour the cream mixture around them. The vegetables should protrude above the sauce. Sprinkle with grated Cheddar cheese.

6 Bake in the oven at 180°C (350°F) mark 4 for 35–40 minutes or until just set. Cool for about 15 minutes before serving warm, garnished with chives and fresh herbs.

Smoked Salmon Quiche

SERVES 6

425 CALORIES/SERVING

75 g (3 oz) butter
white plain flour
salt and pepper
15 ml (1 tbsp) oil
1 large onion, peeled and finely chopped
125 g (4 oz) smoked salmon trimmings
2 eggs
175 g (6 oz) low-fat soft cheese
25 g (1 oz) fresh soft goat's cheese
284 ml (10 fl oz) carton single cream
15 ml (1 level tbsp) chopped fresh thyme or dill

1 First prepare the pastry. Rub the butter into 175 g (6 oz) flour and a pinch of salt as in step 1 of Golden Onion Tart (see page 28). Bind to a dough with about 45 ml (3 tbsp) water. Wrap and chill for 30 minutes.

2 Roll out the pastry, line the tin, chill and bake as in steps 2, 3 and 4 of Golden Onion Tart.

3 Meanwhile, heat the oil in a small pan and sauté the onion until soft and golden. Remove from the heat and leave to cool slightly. Roughly chop the smoked salmon trimmings. Whisk the eggs and cheeses together until almost smooth, then whisk in the cream and herbs. Season with pepper.

4 Scatter the onion and smoked salmon over the base of the flan case and pour over the egg mixture. Bake in the oven at 170°C (325°F) mark 3 for 45–55 minutes or until lightly set. Serve warm or cold.

VARIATION
Use Olive Pastry instead of plain shortcrust (see page 28).

Old-fashioned Pies

These old-fashioned, deep-crust pies have deliciously rich, melt-in-the-mouth fillings, encased in buttery shortcrust pastry.
Simply follow these step-by-step recipes, and you can be sure there will be no leaking sides and no tough fillings – just delicious pies, time after time.

Old-fashioned Steak and Kidney Pie

Serves 8

715 calories/serving

1 kg (2 ¼ lb) piece good-quality stewing beef (i.e. not ready-chopped)
350 g (12 oz) ox kidney
45 ml (3 level tbsp) white plain flour
salt and pepper
about 100 ml (4 fl oz) oil
225 g (8 oz) chopped onion
600 ml (1 pint) beef stock, preferably homemade
150 ml (¼ pint) red wine
15 ml (1 level tbsp) ready-made English mustard
60 ml (4 level tbsp) chopped fresh parsley
125 g (4 oz) button mushrooms, wiped
For the shortcrust pastry
350 g (12 oz) white plain flour
pinch of salt
225 g (8 oz) butter
2 egg yolks
beaten egg, to glaze

1 Cut the beef and kidney into 2.5 cm (1 inch) pieces. Season the flour with salt and pepper, and toss with the beef. Heat the oil in a flameproof casserole, add the beef in batches, and sauté until browned. Return all the beef with any remaining flour to the casserole. Add the onion, kidney, stock, wine and mustard, and bring to the boil. Cover and cook in the oven at 170°C (325°F) mark 3 for about 2 hours. Stir in the chopped parsley, adjust the seasoning and leave to cool.

2 Next make the pastry. Sift the flour and salt into a large mixing bowl. Cut in the butter until pieces about 5 mm (¼ inch) re-main, then rub the butter into the flour with your fingertips until the mixture resembles fine breadcrumbs. Whisk the egg yolks with 45 ml (3 tbsp) water and use to bind the pastry to a firm dough. Knead lightly, wrap and chill for 30 minute–1 hour.

3 Thickly roll out three-quarters of the pastry to a round of about 38 cm (15 inches) in diameter. Carefully fold the pastry over the rolling pin and lift it over and into a 20.5 cm (8 inch) spring-release cake tin. Carefully press the pastry down into the base of the tin and up the sides, allowing excess pastry to flop over the edges of the tin.

4 Strain the juices from the cooked meat and reserve. Layer the meat and the uncooked mushrooms in the lined tin, and pour over 150 ml (¼ pint) meat juices. Put the remaining juices in a saucepan ready to reheat. Roll out the rest of the pastry and use it to top the pie. Pinch the pastry edges to seal well.

5 Trim off excess pastry. Knead the trimmings lightly and re-roll to a thickness of about 5 mm (¼ inch). Cut into leaf shapes, using the back of the knife to mark veins on each one. Arrange the leaves on top of the pie. Make a small hole in the centre of the pie to allow steam to escape. Add a pinch of salt to the beaten egg and brush over the pie. Chill for 30 minutes. Preheat the oven to 200°C (400°F) mark 6.

6 Brush the pie with beaten egg again, and stand it on an edged baking sheet. Bake in the oven for 1 hour, covering with foil to avoid over-browning. Cool for 10 minutes, then carefully remove the side of the tin. Leave the pie on the tin base, and place it on an edged dish. Serve with hot meat juices.

Rich Game Pie (page 34)

Watchpoints

- Make sure that the meat is sufficiently cooked (step 1) or it will be tough and chewy.
- Be careful not to burn the flour when browning the meat as this will make the meat and juices bitter. If meat starts to stick to the pan, add a little more oil.
- The rich shortcrust pastry used in these recipes has more butter to flour than usual, so try not to overwork the pastry or it will be tough and oily. It's important to measure the water carefully – the pastry does not need much liquid.
- Make sure that the pastry does not split when you are lining the tin. Take care to seal the pastry well or the meat juices will run out of the pie when baking. If this happens, the pastry will stick to the tin.

Freezer notes

To freeze: Cool, pack and freeze the meat filling at the end of step 1.
To use: Thaw overnight at cool room temperature and complete as in the recipe.

Rich Game Pie

This pie can be served cold, or you could add 150 ml (¼ pint) meat juices to the pie filling before baking. Cook as directed, then serve the pie warm with the remaining meat juices warmed separately.

SERVES 8

795 CALORIES/SERVING

30 ml (2 level tbsp) white plain flour
salt and pepper
450 g (1 lb) diced casserole venison
125 g (4 oz) rindless streaky bacon
about 60 ml (4 tbsp) oil
225 g (8 oz) chopped onion
600 ml (1 pint) chicken stock
150 ml (¼ pint) port
15 ml (1 level tbsp) redcurrant jelly
5 ml (1 level tsp) dried thyme
1 garlic clove, crushed
60 ml (4 tbsp) orange juice
two pheasants, about 700 g (1½ lb) each
1 quantity shortcrust pastry (see Old-fashioned Steak and Kidney Pie, page 32)
beaten egg, to glaze
5 ml (1 level tsp) powdered gelatine
crisp salad leaves and chunky chutney, to accompany

1 Season the flour with salt and pepper, and toss with the venison. Snip the bacon into small pieces.

2 Heat the oil in a medium flameproof casserole, add the bacon and fry gently until golden. Remove the bacon from the pan with a slotted spoon. Add the venison to the pan in batches and sauté until browned, adding more oil if necessary.

3 Return all the venison to the casserole with any remaining flour. Add the bacon, onion, stock, port, redcurrant jelly, thyme, garlic and orange juice. Bring to the boil, then cover and cook in the oven at 170°C (325°F) mark 3 for 1 hour.

4 Meanwhile, strip all the flesh off the pheasants, discarding skin and bones. Cut the flesh into bite-sized pieces (you'll need about 700 g/1½ lb meat). Add to the casserole after the first hour of cooking time. Bring back to the boil, re-cover and bake for a further 45 minutes or until the meats are quite tender. Adjust the seasoning

and leave to cool. Strain the juices from the meats, reserve and cool (don't chill).

5 Prepare the pastry and use to line a 25.5 × 10 cm (10 × 4 inch) loaf or pie tin with collapsible sides, or a 20.5 cm (8 inch) spring-release cake tin as in steps 2 and 3 of Old-fashioned Steak and Kidney Pie (see page 32). If using the loaf or pie tin, you'll need to roll three-quarters of the pastry to a rectangle about 44 × 33 cm (17½ × 13 inches). Spoon the game mixture into the lined tin with no extra juices. Complete and bake the pie as in steps 4–6 of Old-fashioned Steak and Kidney Pie. It may take a little longer for the pastry sides to brown in the loaf tin. Loosen the tin to check the pastry and, if necessary, refasten the tin sides and return to the oven for a further 15–20 minutes. Cool completely before removing from the tin.

6 In a small bowl, sprinkle the gelatine over 15 ml (1 tbsp) water, and leave to soak for about 5 minutes or until sponge-like in texture. Stand the bowl in a saucepan of simmering water until the gelatine clears and liquefies. Mix with 150 ml (¼ pint) of the cooled, reserved meat juices. Chill until just beginning to set but still liquid.

7 Using a skewer, make four 1 cm (½ inch) holes around the top edge of the pie. Slowly and carefully pour the setting juices into the pie through a 5 mm (¼ inch) piping nozzle or from a jug. Allow them to seep gradually around the meat. Refrigerate to set.

8 Serve with crisp salad leaves and a chunky chutney.

Freezer notes

The meat fillings for both these old-fashioned pies can be frozen after cooking and cooling. Strain off juices after thawing overnight at cool room temperature. Complete the pies as in the recipes.

Golden Pork and Apple Pie

Adding apples to this tasty pork filling helps to keep the pie wonderfully moist.

Serves 8

770 calories/serving

45 ml (3 level tbsp) white plain flour
15 ml (1 level tbsp) ground coriander
5 ml (1 level tsp) ground paprika
salt and pepper
about 1.7 kg (3¾ lb) leg pork (bone in) or 1.1–1.3 kg (2½–2¾ lb) boned weight
125 g (4 oz) rindless streaky bacon
about 75 ml (5 tbsp) oil
600 ml (1 pint) light stock
150 ml (¼ pint) dry white wine
10 ml (2 level tsp) dried sage
450 g (1 lb) leeks
450 g (1 lb) cooking apples
1 quantity shortcrust pastry (see Old-fashioned Steak and Kidney Pie, page 32)
beaten egg, to glaze

1 Mix together the flour, coriander and paprika, and season with salt and pepper. Cut the pork into 2.5 cm (1 inch) pieces, discarding fat and bones. Toss the meat in the seasoned flour. Snip the bacon into small pieces.

2 Heat the oil in a medium flameproof casserole, add the bacon and fry gently until golden. Remove the bacon from the pan with a slotted spoon. Add the pork to the pan in batches and sauté until browned, adding a little more oil if necessary.

3 Return all the pork to the casserole with any remaining flour. Add the bacon, stock, wine and sage, and bring to the boil. Cover and bake in the oven at 170°C (325°F) mark 3 for 45 minutes.

4 Meanwhile, trim, rinse, drain and slice the leeks into 1 cm (½ inch) thick pieces. Peel, quarter, core and thickly slice the apples. Add the leeks and apples to the casserole, re-cover and bake for another 45 minutes or until the meat is quite tender. Adjust the seasoning to taste, cool completely, then carefully strain the juices from the cooked meat and set aside.

5 Prepare the shortcrust pastry and use it to line a 20.5 cm (8 inch) spring-release cake tin as in steps 2 and 3 of Old-fashioned Steak and Kidney Pie (see page 32). Carefully spoon the pork mixture into the prepared tin and pour over 150 ml (¼ pint) of the meat juices. Put the remaining meat juices in a saucepan ready to reheat when required.

6 Complete as in steps 4–6 of Old-fashioned Steak and Kidney Pie.

Puff Pastry

The richest of all the pastries, puff requires patience, practice and very light handling. The light layered texture of puff pastry is achieved by rolling and folding the dough to trap pockets of air between the layers.

Makes 450 g (1 lb)

270 calories/25 g (1 oz)

450 g (1 lb) strong plain flour
pinch of salt
450 g (1 lb) butter or margarine, chilled
15 ml (1 tbsp) lemon juice

1 Mix the flour and salt together in a bowl. Cut off 50 g (2 oz) of the butter and flatten the remaining butter with a rolling pin to a slab 2 cm (¾ inch) thick.

2 Cut the 50 g (2 oz) butter into small pieces, add to the flour and rub in. Using a round-bladed knife, stir in the lemon juice and about 300 ml (½ pint) chilled water or sufficient to make a soft, elastic dough.

3 Quickly knead the dough until smooth, and shape into a round. Cut through half the depth in the shape of a cross. Open out to form a star.

4 Roll out, keeping the centre four times as thick as the flaps. Place the slab of butter in the centre of the dough.

5 Fold the flaps envelope-style over the butter, and press gently with a rolling pin. Roll out to a rectangle measuring about 40 × 20.5 cm (16 × 8 inches).

6 Fold the bottom third up and the top third down, keeping the edges straight. Press the edges to seal. Wrap in greaseproof paper and 'rest' in the refrigerator for 30 minutes.

7 Put the pastry on a lightly floured work surface with the folded edges to the sides, then repeat the rolling, folding and resting sequence five times.

Note
Shape the pastry as required, then leave to rest in the refrigerator for 30 minutes before baking. Brush with beaten egg and bake at 220°C (425°F) mark 7, unless otherwise stated.

Watchpoints
• Remember to rest the pastry in the refrigerator for 30 minutes after making and again after shaping.
• Strong plain flour helps to give the pastry a light, open structure.

• Whenever possible, puff pastry should be made the day before use. It is not practical to make it in a quantity with less than 450 g (1 lb) flour. This quantity is equivalent to two 375 g (13 oz) packets.

Freezer notes
To freeze: Pack in amounts that are practical to thaw and use.
To use: Thaw at cool room temperature for 1½–2 hours.

Sausage Rolls

MAKES 28

230 CALORIES/ROLL

1 quantity Puff Pastry (see left)
450 g (1 lb) pork sausagemeat
flour, for dusting
a little milk
beaten egg, to glaze

1 On a lightly floured surface, roll out half the pastry to a 40 × 20.5 cm (16 × 8 inch) oblong. Cut lengthways into two strips. Divide the sausagemeat into four pieces, dust with flour and form into rolls the length of the pastry. Lay a sausagemeat roll on each pastry strip.

2 Repeat with the remaining pastry and sausagemeat rolls. Brush the pastry edges with a little milk, fold one side of the pastry over the sausagemeat and press the two long edges firmly together to seal.

3 Brush the pastry with egg, then cut each roll diagonally into 5 cm (2 inch) lengths. Make three small cuts in the top of each sausage roll. Place on a baking sheet and bake in the oven at 220°C (425°F) mark 7 for 15 minutes. Reduce the temperature to 180°C (350°F) mark 4 and cook for a further 15 minutes. Serve hot or cold.

Mushroom and Pepper Vol-au-Vents

MAKES 8

770 CALORIES/SERVING

1 quantity Puff Pastry (see page 36)
beaten egg, to glaze
For the filling
2 yellow peppers, halved and deseeded
2 red peppers, halved and deseeded
60 ml (4 tbsp) olive oil
75 g (3 oz) shallots, peeled and finely chopped
1 large garlic clove, crushed
90 ml (6 tbsp) white wine
700 g (1½ lb) mixed mushrooms (such as chanterelles, brown cap, button), wiped and thickly sliced
90 ml (6 tbsp) double cream
15 ml (1 level tbsp) chopped fresh tarragon or 5 ml (1 level tsp) dried tarragon
salt and pepper
fresh herbs and salad leaves, to garnish

1 Roll out the pastry on a lightly floured surface to 1 cm (½ inch) thick. Using a 9 cm (3½ inch) pastry cutter, or a sharp knife and a ramekin as a guide, cut out eight rounds.

2 Place on a dampened baking sheet. Using a 6 cm (2½ inch) cutter or a sharp knife, cut an inner oval or round halfway through the pastry and 1 cm (½ inch) in from the edge.

3 Lightly score a lattice on the surface of the pastry. Brush the tops with beaten egg and chill for 30 minutes. Bake in the oven at 230°C (450°F) mark 8 for 10 minutes, then at 200°C (400°F) mark 6 for 10–15 minutes or until well risen and golden brown.

4 Cut around the lids of the vol-au-vents, lift off and scoop out the soft dough inside. Reserve the lids. Cover the vol-au-vents lightly with foil and return to the oven for a further 10 minutes or until dried out and crisp. Keep warm, covered, in a low oven.

5 Place the pepper halves, skin-side up, under a hot grill for about 15 minutes or until soft and well charred. Peel off the skin under cold running water, then pat the peppers dry with absorbent kitchen paper and slice thinly.

6 Heat the oil in a large saucepan and sauté the shallots and garlic for 1–2 minutes. Add the wine and boil to reduce by half. Add the mushrooms and sauté for 5 minutes. Add the peppers and cream, bring to the boil and bubble for 2–3 minutes. Add the tarragon, and season with salt and pepper. Spoon into the vol-au-vent cases and replace the lids. Garnish and serve.

Note

These vol-au-vents can be made with ready-made puff pastry if preferred. Use two 375 g (13 oz) packets and roll out more thinly – to a 5 mm (¼ inch) thickness – to allow for extra rise.

Spinach and Seafood Pasties

SERVES 4

660 CALORIES/SERVING

4 cod steaks, about 125 g (4 oz) each
40 g (1½ oz) butter or margarine
350 g (12 oz) frozen spinach, thawed
30 ml (2 tbsp) lemon juice
freshly grated nutmeg
15 g (½ oz) white plain flour
150 ml (¼ pint) milk
salt and pepper
2 eggs, hard-boiled and roughly chopped
125 g (4 oz) cooked peeled prawns
30 ml (2 level tbsp) chopped fresh parsley
I quantity Puff Pastry (see page 36)
beaten egg, to glaze
watercress sprigs, to garnish

1 Skin the cod steaks and carefully remove the central bones.
2 Melt 25 g (1 oz) butter in a saucepan. Add the spinach and cook over a high heat, stirring frequently, until all excess moisture has evaporated. Remove from the heat and stir in the lemon juice and a generous grating of nutmeg.
3 Melt the remaining butter in a saucepan, stir in the flour and cook for 1 minute. Remove from the heat and gradually stir in the milk, then bring to the boil, stirring. Season with salt and pepper, reduce the heat and simmer, stirring, for 1–2 minutes. Stir in the eggs, prawns and parsley, then leave to cool slightly.
4 Divide the pastry into four equal pieces. Roll out each piece to a large square, about 23 cm (9 inches). Place a cod steak on one half of each pastry square. Cover with the spinach and top with the prawn sauce.
5 Brush the pastry edges with beaten egg and fold the pastry over the fish to enclose completely, tucking the edges under each parcel to neaten. With a sharp knife, carefully score the pastry in one direction only. Place on a baking sheet and brush with beaten egg.
6 Bake in the oven at 220°C (425°F) mark 7 for 25 minutes or until the pastry is crisp and browned. Serve immediately, garnished with watercress.

Puff Pastry Mince Pies

These are definitely plate rather than finger pies as the light puff pastry tends to flake the moment you bite into it.

MAKES ABOUT 12 PIES

425 CALORIES/PIE

25 g (1 oz) walnuts, chopped
25 g (1 oz) Brazil nuts, chopped
about 150 g (5 oz) mincemeat
I quantity Puff Pastry (see page 36)
caster sugar, to dust
crème fraîche or single cream, to serve

1 Stir the chopped nuts into the mincemeat.
2 Roll out the pastry very thinly – you might find this easier to do in two batches. Stamp out about twelve 10 cm (4 inch) rounds and twelve 9 cm (3½ inch) rounds.
3 Place the smaller puff pastry rounds on baking sheets and carefully spoon about 15 ml (1 level tbsp) mincemeat on to the centre of each one. Moisten the exposed pastry edges with a little water.
4 Top with the larger pastry circles, pressing the edges firmly together to seal. If wished, you can neaten the edges by pressing a 7.5–9 cm (3–3½ inch) cutter over each pie. Make a small hole in the top of each pie for the steam to escape. Chill for about 15 minutes.
5 Bake in the oven at 220°C (425°F) mark 7 for about 15 minutes or until well browned and risen. Serve the pies warm and lightly dusted with caster sugar. If you wish, serve with crème fraîche or single cream.

Freezer notes
To freeze: Leave the pies to cool, then pack and freeze.
To use: Put frozen pies on a baking sheet, cover loosely with foil, and reheat in the oven at 200°C (400°F) mark 6 for 15 minutes.

Choux Pastry

Choux pastry is unlike any other pastry as it is cooked twice. At the first attempt, it can be quite alarming to make – when the flour is added it will look very lumpy, but don't panic as it will beat to a smooth and shiny paste. The paste can be made the day before if you keep it covered in the refrigerator.

Profiteroles

SERVES 6

640 CALORIES/SERVING

For the choux pastry

65 g (2½ oz) white plain flour

pinch of salt

50 g (2 oz) butter, diced

2 eggs (size 2)

For the chocolate sauce

225 g (8 oz) plain chocolate

142 ml (5 fl oz) carton double cream

orange-flavoured liqueur, to taste

sugar (optional)

To finish

284 ml (10 fl oz) carton double cream

icing sugar, for dusting

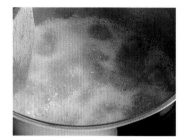

1 To make the choux pastry, sift the flour with the salt on to a sheet of greaseproof paper. Place the butter in a small saucepan with 150 ml (¼ pint) water. Heat gently until the butter melts, then bring to a rapid boil. Remove from the heat and immediately tip in all the flour, beating until smooth. Leave to cool for about 10 minutes.

2 Lightly whisk the eggs together. Add a little at a time to the flour mixture, beating well after each addition. Ensure that the mixture becomes thick and shiny before adding any more egg – if it is added too quickly, the choux pastry will become runny and the cooked buns will be flat.

3 Lightly moisten one baking sheet. Using two damp teaspoons, spoon about 18 small mounds of the choux pastry on to the baking sheet, allowing each one room to spread out and rise. Alternatively, spoon the choux pastry into a piping bag fitted with a 1 cm (½ inch) plain nozzle and pipe the mixture on to the baking sheet.

4 Bake in the oven at 220°C (425°F) mark 7 for about 25 minutes or until well risen, crisp and golden brown. Make a small hole in the side of each bun to allow the steam to escape, then return them to the oven for a further 5 minutes or until thoroughly dried out. Slide on to wire racks to cool.

5 To make the sauce, break up the chocolate and place it in a medium saucepan with the cream and 60 ml (4 tbsp) water. Heat gently, stirring occasionally, until the chocolate melts to a smooth sauce. Do not boil. Remove from the heat.

6 To finish, lightly whip the cream until it just holds its shape. Pipe into the choux buns or split open the buns and spoon in the cream. Just before serving, gently reheat the sauce. Add a little liqueur to taste and, if liked, some sugar. Dust the buns lightly with icing sugar, and serve with the sauce.

Freezer notes
To freeze: Baked, unfilled choux pastry will freeze.
To use: Place frozen on baking sheets and thaw in a hot oven for 5 minutes. Cool, then complete the recipe.

Watchpoints
• Don't let the water boil before the butter melts or it will evaporate. It is this water turning to steam that helps to make the choux buns rise.

• Slowly add the beaten eggs, making sure that the choux pastry is thick, smooth and shiny after each addition. If the choux pastry starts to thin down and refuses to thicken despite constant beat-

ing, a small amount of beaten egg can be omitted.
• Bake one large baking sheet of choux pastry at a time to ensure even rising.
• Don't be tempted to open the oven door while the

choux buns are baking; if they have not set, the dough will flatten.
• Always pierce the cooked buns to allow the steam to escape, then return to the oven to dry out properly.

Coffee and Caramel Eclairs

MAKES ABOUT 36

75 CALORIES/ECLAIR

For the choux pastry

65 g (2½ oz) white plain flour

pinch of salt

50 g (2 oz) butter, diced

2 eggs (size 2)

To finish

175 g (6 oz) granulated sugar

284 ml (10 fl oz) carton double cream

60 ml (4 tbsp) Tia Maria

1 Prepare the choux pastry as in steps 1 and 2 of Profiteroles (see page 40).
2 Lightly moisten a baking sheet. Spoon the choux pastry into a piping bag fitted with a 1 cm (½ inch) plain nozzle, and pipe out 36 small éclair shapes, each one about 4–5 cm (1½–2 inches) long.
3 Bake in the oven for about 20 minutes and cool as in step 4 of Profiteroles.
4 Place 50 g (2 oz) granulated sugar in a small saucepan and heat gently until the sugar dissolves and caramelizes. Do not stir, but occasionally prod the sugar gently to help it dissolve evenly. Remove from the heat as soon as the sugar caramelizes.
5 Carefully dip the tops of the éclairs into the caramel and place on a wire rack to set. Take great care not to touch the caramel as it can cause a painful burn. This amount of caramel will top about one-third of the éclairs. Repeat with the remaining sugar until all the éclairs are coated.
6 Lightly whip the cream until it just begins to hold its shape. Gradually whip in the Tia Maria.
7 Split open the éclairs and fill with the coffee cream. Leave in a cool place for up to 2 hours before serving.

Chocolate Croquembouche

This classic French gâteau of a tower of choux buns is traditionally assembled with caramel, but this isn't really necessary. As long as the pyramid has a wide base, it won't collapse.

SERVES 12

630 CALORIES/SERVING

For the choux pastry

100 g (3¾ oz) white plain flour

pinch of salt

7.5 ml (1½ level tsp) cocoa powder

75 g (3 oz) butter

3 eggs (size 2)

To assemble

225 g (8 oz) shortcrust pastry (prepared weight), see page 28

75 g (3 oz) almonds, unskinned

75 g (3 oz) granulated sugar

450 ml (15 fl oz) double cream

icing sugar, to decorate

For the chocolate fudge sauce

350 g (12 oz) plain chocolate

200 ml (7 fl oz) double cream

60 ml (4 level tbsp) soft light brown sugar

1 Prepare the choux pastry as in steps 1 and 2 of Profiteroles (see page 40), sifting the cocoa powder with the flour and using 225 ml (8 fl oz) water.

2 Continue as in steps 3 and 4 of Profiteroles, making about 40 choux buns (you will need to use two baking sheets). Bake each sheet of choux buns separately in the oven for about 20 minutes.

3 Roll out the shortcrust pastry to a 21.5–23 cm (8½–9 inch) round. Place on a baking sheet and crimp the edges. Prick lightly and bake in the oven at 190°C (375°F) mark 5 for about 20 minutes or until golden brown. Cool on a wire rack.

4 Place the almonds and granulated sugar in a medium frying pan. Heat gently until the sugar dissolves and caramelizes. Gently move the nuts around the pan to prevent them from burning. Pour out on to an oiled baking sheet and leave to cool and set. Grind in a food processor or through a nut mouli to form a coarse praline.

5 Lightly whip the cream and fold in the ground praline. Split open the choux buns and fill with the cream.

6 Place the shortcrust pastry on a flat plate. Carefully pile the choux buns into a pyramid shape. Refrigerate for up to 2 hours before serving.

7 Prepare the chocolate fudge sauce as in step 5 of Profiteroles, adding the sugar and 90 ml (6 tbsp) water to the chocolate and cream in the saucepan.

8 To serve, dust the buns with icing sugar and drizzle over some of the warm chocolate fudge sauce. Serve the remaining sauce separately.

Freezer notes
The baked, unfilled choux buns can be frozen and used as for Profiteroles (see page 40).

Gougère

SERVES 4

780 CALORIES/SERVING

For the choux pastry

100 g (3¾ oz) white plain flour
pinch of salt
pinch of cayenne
75 g (3 oz) butter
3 eggs (size 2)
75 g (3 oz) mature Cheddar cheese, grated
30 ml (2 level tbsp) chopped fresh parsley
For the filling
25 g (1 oz) butter
1 onion, peeled and chopped
1 garlic clove, crushed
125 g (4 oz) mushrooms, wiped and sliced
300 ml (½ pint) thick Béchamel Sauce (see page 14)
350 g (12 oz) cooked boneless chicken, chopped
30 ml (2 level tbsp) chopped fresh parsley
salt and pepper
15–30 ml (1–2 tbsp) fresh breadcrumbs
30 ml (2 level tbsp) freshly grated Parmesan cheese

1 To make the filling, melt the butter in a saucepan, add the onion and garlic, and fry for about 5 minutes or until softened. Add the mushrooms and cook for 2–3 minutes or until softened. Stir in the Béchamel Sauce. Leave to cool.

2 Prepare the choux pastry as in steps 1 and 2 of Profiteroles (see page 40), using 200 ml (7 fl oz) water and folding in the cheese and parsley after adding the eggs.

3 Spoon the choux pastry around the edge of a greased gratin dish. Bake in the oven at 200°C (400°F) mark 6 for about 25 minutes or until well risen and golden brown. Meanwhile, add the chicken to the cold sauce with the parsley and seasoning.

4 Pile the filling in the centre of the choux ring. Sprinkle with the breadcrumbs and Parmesan and bake in the oven for a further 15 minutes or until the filling is hot. Serve immediately.

Pâte Sucrée

Pâte sucrée is the classic rich, crisp pastry used for sweet French pâtisserie. When baked, the pastry is thin, crisp, yet melting in texture; it keeps its shape, shrinks very little and does not spread during baking. Traditionally the pastry is mixed on the work surface, but it is easier and much less messy to make it in a bowl.

Three-Fruit Tart

We've allowed plenty of pastry for easier handling. Use the trimmings for biscuits.

SERVES 6

470 CALORIES/SERVING

For the pâte sucrée

175 g (6 oz) white plain flour

pinch of salt

75 g (3 oz) unsalted butter, diced

75 g (3 oz) caster sugar

1 egg (size 1 or 2), beaten

For the filling

142 ml (5 fl oz) carton double cream

10 ml (2 level tsp) icing sugar

60 ml (4 level tbsp) fromage frais, soured cream or natural yogurt

juice and finely grated rind of 1 orange

450 g (1 lb) mixed berries, such as raspberries, small strawberries and blueberries

about 150 ml (10 level tbsp) redcurrant jelly

1 Sift the flour and salt together into a bowl. Rub in the butter until the mixture resembles breadcrumbs. Don't overwork or it will become sticky. Mix in the sugar. Pour in the egg and, using a blunt-edged knife, cut the ingredients together until mixed. Using one hand, gradually knead the pastry together, then turn out on to a floured work surface and knead until smooth. Wrap in cling film. Chill for 30 minutes – 1 hour.

2 Dust the work surface with a little flour. Roll out the pastry quite thinly to an oblong large enough to line a 34 × 11.5 cm (13½ × 4½ inch) loose-based tart tin. To make sure the pastry doesn't stick to the work surface, occasionally move the dough around. Lightly flour the rolling pin and loosely roll the pastry over it, starting from a long edge. Carefully unroll over the tin.

3 Ease the pastry into the tart tin, pressing it right down into the corners and up the sides. Move the rolling pin back and forth across the top to cut off the excess pastry. (Reserve the trimmings to bake into biscuits.) Press the pastry into the flutes around the sides of the tin, and neaten the top edge. Chill for at least 30 minutes or freeze for 10 minutes only.

4 Prick the pastry base with a fork, then line with greaseproof paper. Fill with baking beans. Bake at 200°C (400°F) mark 6 for 12–15 minutes or until the pastry is set. Remove the beans and paper, and return the pastry to the oven at 180°C (350°F) mark 4 for 10–12 minutes or until golden brown. Cool in the tin.

5 To complete the tart, lightly whip the cream with the icing sugar until it just holds its shape, then fold in the fromage frais and orange rind. Spoon into the pastry case. Pick over the fruit and pile on top of the cream.

6 Beat the redcurrant jelly until almost smooth, then heat with 30 ml (2 tbsp) orange juice. Sieve and leave to cool slightly, then brush over the fruit. Serve the tart within 2 hours of completing it, or the creamy filling will soften the pastry too much.

Individual Fruit Flans (page 47)

Watchpoints

• You can prepare pâte sucrée in a food processor, but don't overwork it. Process the butter, flour and sugar, then add the egg until just blended. Knead on the work surface.

• If the pastry is soft, sticky and difficult to roll out, you may have rubbed in the butter too much, or the dough may not have

been sufficiently chilled. Knead in a little extra flour.

• Don't overknead the dough in step 1, or the pastry will be tough and hard. Baking it for too long will cause the sugar to caramelize, giving the same hard result.

• Don't use too much flour when you knead and roll out the dough, or the pastry will look streaky and cracked.

• Flour the rolling pin frequently to prevent small particles of pastry sticking to it and pitting the dough.

• To prevent the pastry from shrinking while cooking, ease it gently into the corners of the tin, making sure you don't stretch it. Check the pastry is set before removing the paper and baking beans.

Freezer notes

To freeze: Overwrap and freeze at the end of step 4.
To use: Unwrap and thaw at cool room temperature for about 2 hours.

Tarte au Citron

SERVES 6

550 CALORIES/SERVING

I quantity Pâte Sucrée (see page 44)
For the filling
3 eggs, beaten
150 g (5 oz) caster sugar
3 lemons
25 g (I oz) butter
For the decoration
150 g (5 oz) caster sugar
2 lemons
90 ml (6 level tbsp) apricot jam
soured cream, to accompany (optional)

1 Prepare the pâte sucrée as in step 1 of Three-Fruit Tart (see page 44). Roll out and use to line a tranche tin or 23 cm (9 inch) base measurement fluted flan tin. Bake blind as in step 4 of Three-Fruit Flan, but once the baking beans and paper have been removed, return to the oven for 7–8 minutes only.

2 Meanwhile, prepare the filling. Place the eggs, sugar, grated rind of 1 lemon and the strained juice of all 3 lemons in a medium heatproof bowl. Whisk until evenly mixed. Set the bowl over a pan of simmering water and heat until the mixture thickens slightly, whisking occasionally. (Do not overheat, or the mixture will curdle.) Take off the heat and whisk in the butter.

3 Pour the mixture into the pastry case and bake in the oven at 200°C (400°F) mark 6 for about 15 minutes or until just set. Leave to cool, then ease out of the tin.

4 Meanwhile, prepare the lemon slices for the decoration. Put the sugar and 120 ml (4½ fl oz) water in a saucepan and heat gently until the sugar has dissolved. Bring to the boil and boil for 1 minute. Cut the lemons in half lengthways, then slice finely, discarding the pips. Place in the hot syrup and bring back to the boil. Remove from the heat, pour into a bowl and leave to soak for at least 2 hours.

5 Drain the lemon slices and arrange over the tart. Boil the jam with 15 ml (1 tbsp) water. Sieve and cool, then brush over the tart and leave to set. Serve with soured cream, if wished.

Cook's tip

The lemon filling can be made ahead. At the end of step 2, cover the surface with damp greaseproof paper. Cool and refrigerate for up to 3 days. Stir before spooning into the pastry case and completing the recipe.

Tarte aux Abricots

SERVES 6

580 CALORIES/SERVING

50 g (2 oz) butter, softened
50 g (2 oz) caster sugar
50 g (2 oz) ground almonds
few drops of vanilla essence
I egg, beaten
10 ml (2 tsp) rum
I quantity Pâte Sucrée (see page 44)
two 420 g (14 oz) cans apricot halves
90 ml (6 level tbsp) apricot jam
single cream, to accompany (optional)

1 Beat together the butter and sugar until well blended. Mix in the almonds and vanilla essence, followed by the egg, beating well. Add the rum. Cover and chill.

2 Prepare the pâte sucrée as in step 1 of Three-Fruit Tart (see page 44). Roll out and use to line a 23 cm (9 inch) base measurement fluted flan tin. Prick the base of the pastry all over with a fork.

3 Drain the apricots and dry on absorbent kitchen paper. Spread the almond mixture in the pastry case and top with three-quarters of the apricots (use the remainder in fruit salads, etc.). Bake in the oven at 190°C (375°F) mark 5 for 40–45 minutes or until golden brown and firm to the touch. Cool slightly, then remove from the tin.

4 Boil the apricot jam with 15 ml (1 tbsp) water. Sieve, leave to cool slightly, then brush over the tart. Leave to set. Serve with single cream, if wished.

Individual Fruit Flans

MAKES 10

385 CALORIES/SERVING

For the pâte sucrée

225 g (8 oz) white plain flour

pinch of salt

125 g (4 oz) unsalted butter, diced

125 g (4 oz) caster sugar

4 egg yolks, beaten

For the apricot glaze

225 g (8 oz) apricot jam

15 ml (1 tbsp) kirsch

For the filling

300 ml (½ pint) Crème Pâtissière (see right)

selection of seasonal fruits, such as raspberries, strawberries, blueberries, figs, grapes and kiwi fruit

1 Prepare the pâte sucrée as in step 1 of Three-Fruit Tart (see page 44). Roll out the pastry on a lightly floured surface and cut out ten 12 cm (5 inch) circles with a plain cutter. Use to line individual 10 cm (4 inch) loose-based fluted flan tins. Prick the bases with a fork, then chill for 30 minutes.

2 Line the pastry cases with foil or greaseproof paper and fill with baking beans. Bake blind in the oven at 190°C (375°F) mark 5 for about 20 minutes or until golden and crisp. Allow the flan cases to cool a little in the tins, then carefully remove from the tins and leave to cool completely on a wire rack.

3 To make the apricot glaze, put the jam and kirsch in a saucepan with 15 ml (1 tbsp) water, and heat gently until melted. Simmer for 1 minute, then sieve. Brush the inside of each pastry case evenly with glaze.

4 Spread a generous layer of crème pâtissière in each pastry case. Arrange the sliced or whole fruit on top.

5 Reheat the remaining apricot glaze, then carefully brush over the fruits to glaze evenly. Serve as soon as possible.

Crème Pâtissière

To make 300 ml (½ pint) Crème Pâtissière, heat 300 ml (½ pint) milk with a split vanilla pod almost to the boil, then set aside to infuse. Whisk 3 egg yolks and 50 g (2 oz) caster sugar together in a bowl until pale and thick. Whisk in 30 ml (2 level tbsp) each plain flour and cornflour. Strain in the milk, whisking constantly. Return to the pan, bring to the boil and cook, whisking, for 2–3 minutes or until thickened. Pour into a bowl and cool, with a circle of damp greaseproof paper on top to prevent a skin forming. When cool, fold in one stiffly whisked egg white.

EGGS

For versatility and convenience in everyday cooking, eggs are hard to beat, but they also feature strongly in some essential cookery techniques – the making of pancakes, omelettes, soufflés and meringue. They are used to lighten, bind, thicken, enrich and set countless dishes, both sweet and savoury, and are an essential ingredient of emulsified sauces and custards.

Too often treated as mundane, a good omelette is endlessly versatile. As well as many suggested omelette fillings, this chapter includes two variations on the omelette – a Spanish tortilla and a frittata – both satisfying meals in themselves. Pancakes, too, can be filled with various sweet or savoury ingredients to make delicious hot dishes or desserts. Though the results are very different, hot soufflés and meringues depend on the fluffy whiteness of whisked egg white for their individual characteristic textures. In this chapter, you will find a good selection of both soufflés and meringue recipes from which to choose.

Omelettes

With care, anyone can master the art of omelette making. Delicate handling and a little practice is needed – don't be discouraged if your first two or three omelettes are not successful. Two good points about omelettes are the short preparation time and the way they can be combined with cooked meat, fish or vegetables – either in the omelette itself, as a filling, or as an accompaniment.

SERVES 1

390 CALORIES/SERVING

2–3 eggs

salt and pepper

15 ml (1 tbsp) milk or water

butter or margarine for cooking

1 Whisk the eggs just enough to break them down; over-beating spoils the texture of the omelette. Season with salt and pepper and add the milk or water.

2 Place an omelette or non-stick frying pan over a gentle heat and, when it is hot, add a generous knob of butter and heat until it is foaming but not brown.

3 Add the beaten eggs. Stir gently with a fork or wooden spatula, drawing the mixture from the sides to the centre as it sets and letting the liquid egg in the centre run to the sides. When the eggs have set, stop stirring and cook for a further 30 seconds–1 minute or until the omelette is golden brown underneath and still creamy on top. Don't overcook or it will be tough.

4 If making a filled omelette, add the filling at this point. Tilt the pan away from you slightly and use a palette knife to fold over a third of the omelette to the centre, then fold over the opposite third. Slide the omelette out on to a warmed plate, letting it flip over so that the folded sides are underneath. Serve at once.

Watchpoints

• Have everything ready before beginning to make an omelette, including a heated plate on which to serve it.

• A good omelette should be cooked in no more than 2 minutes; both slow cooking and overcooking make an omelette tough.

• Undoubtedly, when cooking omelettes, butter gives the best flavour, but margarine or oil can be used as a substitute. Bacon fat can also be used.

• Gently heat the pan before use to ensure that it is heated evenly right to the edges – a fierce heat would cause the pan to heat unevenly.

Omelette pans

Special omelette pans are obtainable and should be kept for omelettes only. If you do not own such a pan, a heavy-based frying pan can also be used. Non-stick pans are ideal for omelettes and do not require 'seasoning' before use (see page 59). Whether of cast-iron, copper, enamelled iron or aluminium, the pan should be thick, so that it will hold sufficient heat to cook the egg mixture as soon as it is put in.

OMELETTE FILLINGS

Fines Herbes
Add 15 ml (1 level tbsp) finely chopped fresh chervil, chives and tarragon or a large pinch of dried mixed herbs to the egg before cooking.

Tomato
Skin and chop 1–2 tomatoes and fry in a little butter for 5 minutes or until soft and pulpy. Put in the centre of the omelette before folding.

Cheese
Grate 40 g (1½ oz) cheese. Sprinkle half on the omelette before folding, and the rest over the finished omelette.

Mushroom
Thickly slice about 50 g (2 oz) mushrooms and cook in butter until soft. Put in the centre of the omelette before folding. (When available, use wild mushrooms.)

Curried Vegetable
Roughly chop leftover vegetables, such as potato, green beans, broad beans or parsnips. Fry in oil with about 2.5 ml (½ level tsp) curry powder and a little crushed garlic. Put in the centre of the omelette before folding.

Lovage and Blue Cheese
Add 10 ml (2 level tsp) finely chopped fresh lovage to the beaten egg mixture. Cut 25–50 g (1–2 oz) Blue Cheshire, Blue Stilton or Blue Wensleydale cheese into thin slices and scatter over the omelette before folding.

Goat's Cheese
Soften about 25 g (1 oz) mild goat's cheese and blend with a little fromage frais. Season with salt and pepper and put in the centre of the omelette before folding.

Prawn
Allow 50 g (2 oz) cooked peeled prawns per omelette. Sprinkle the prawns and a little chopped fresh tarragon in the centre of the omelette before folding.

Smoked Salmon
Combine 25 g (1 oz) chopped smoked salmon with a little chopped fresh dill and 15 ml (1 tbsp) soured cream. Put in the centre of the omelette before folding over.

Frittata

SERVES 6

215 CALORIES/SERVING

125 g (4 oz) small new potatoes

125 g (4 oz) shelled broad beans

salt and pepper

50 g (2 oz) soft cheese, preferably fresh goat's cheese

4 eggs

30 ml (2 level tbsp) chopped fresh thyme

30 ml (2 tbsp) olive oil

1 onion, peeled and roughly chopped

225 g (8 oz) courgettes, sliced

125 g (4 oz) cooked peeled prawns

125 g (4 oz) lightly cooked salmon, flaked

whole cooked prawns, to garnish

1 Cook the potatoes and broad beans separately in boiling salted water until just tender. Drain thoroughly.
2 In a bowl, whisk together the cheese, eggs, thyme and seasoning.
3 Heat the oil in a large shallow flameproof pan. Add the onion, courgettes, potatoes and beans, and cook, stirring, for 2–3 minutes, then add the prawns and salmon. Pour in the egg mixture.
4 As the egg cooks, push the mixture into the centre of the pan to allow the raw egg to flow down to the edge.

When the frittata is lightly set, place the pan under a hot grill for 2–3 minutes or until golden. Garnish with prawns and serve immediately.

VARIATIONS

Substitute fresh sorrel for the thyme. The broad beans can be skinned for extra colour.

Spinach and Mushroom Omelette

SERVES 2

490 CALORIES/SERVING

225 g (8 oz) freshly cooked spinach, or frozen chopped spinach, thawed

4 eggs

1.25 ml (¼ level tsp) freshly grated nutmeg

salt and pepper

40 g (1½ oz) butter or margarine

125 g (4 oz) button mushrooms, wiped and thinly sliced

10 ml (2 level tsp) wholegrain mustard

150 ml (¼ pint) soured cream

1 Put the spinach in a sieve or colander and press with the back of a spoon to remove excess liquid. Place in a blender with the eggs and nutmeg. Season with salt and pepper, and blend until smooth.
2 Heat 25 g (1 oz) butter in a large non-stick frying pan. When foaming, add the spinach mixture and cook until the base is set, drawing the mixture from the sides to the centre as it sets, and allowing the liquid egg to run to the edge of the pan to cook. Once the base is firm, place under a hot grill for 1–2 minutes.
3 Meanwhile, heat the remaining butter in a pan and sauté the mushrooms with the mustard. Add the soured cream, season with salt and pepper, and bring to the boil.
4 Spoon the mushroom mixture over one half of the omelette, then flip over the other half to enclose the filling. Serve immediately.

Omelette Rolls

These make a delicious alternative to sandwiches. Serve them cold, thickly sliced, on a bed of fresh parsley.

MAKES ABOUT 8 OMELETTES

85 CALORIES/OMELETTE PLUS FILLING

8 eggs
salt and pepper
chopped mixed fresh herbs (optional)
butter for cooking

1 Lightly whisk the eggs with 60 ml (4 tbsp) water. Season with salt and pepper, and add some fresh herbs, if wished.

2 Heat a little butter in a large non-stick frying pan. Add a small ladle of the egg mixture and swirl it around the pan to give a thin layer. Cook over a gentle heat for about 30 seconds or until set and brown underneath.

3 Loosen the omelette around the edges, then turn it out on to a sheet of greaseproof paper. Cook a further seven omelettes in the same way, stacking them one on top of the other, interleaved with greaseproof paper. Cover and leave to cool.

4 Once cool, spread each of the omelettes with one of the savoury fillings suggested below, and roll up. Cover tightly and refrigerate until required.

SAVOURY FILLINGS

Chicken and Watercress
Mix chopped cooked chicken with roughly chopped watercress and a little mayonnaise. Season with salt and pepper, and add a little Dijon mustard.

Prawn Mayonnaise
Mix small cooked peeled prawns with garlic mayonnaise, chopped cucumber and a little grated lemon rind and juice. Season to taste.

Salami and Cheese
Use thinly sliced salami or ham. Top with a little soft cheese and some shredded salad leaves.

Crunchy Vegetable
Coarsely grate some carrot, fennel and celery. Mix with a little yogurt, lemon juice and wholegrain mustard. Add chopped parsley and grated cheese to taste.

Tomato and Radish
Roughly chop tomatoes and radishes and roll inside the omelettes with salad leaves and a dash of lemon mayonnaise or Greek yogurt.

Smoked Fish
Flake smoked trout or mackerel fillet and mix with mayonnaise, a dash of lemon or lime juice, and a generous dollop of creamed horseradish. Add some finely chopped cucumber or apple.

Herb Tortilla

The potatoes need to be finely sliced for this Spanish version of an omelette – the slicing blade of a food processor is ideal.

SERVES 4

280 CALORIES/SERVING

olive oil
175 g (6 oz) onion, peeled and sliced
450 g (1 lb) old potatoes, thinly sliced
4 eggs
5 ml (1 level tsp) chopped fresh tarragon or 2.5 ml (½ level tsp) dried tarragon
60 ml (4 level tbsp) chopped fresh parsley
salt and pepper
tarragon, to garnish (optional)

1 Heat 30 ml (2 tbsp) oil in a large non-stick frying pan. Add the onions and cook for 5–6 minutes or until beginning to soften.

2 Add the potatoes to the pan and cook over a moderate heat, stirring frequently, for 10–15 minutes or until the potatoes are golden and almost tender.

3 Whisk the eggs with the herbs in a large bowl. Season with salt and pepper and stir in the potatoes and onions. Set aside the mixture and wash out the frying pan.

4 Heat a fine film of oil in the clean pan. Return all the ingredients to the pan and press down gently. Cook for 4–5 minutes or until the egg is nearly set.

5 Brown the tortilla under the grill. Garnish with tarragon if liked, and serve warm or cold, cut into wedges.

Hot Soufflés

Hot soufflés are made from a rich creamy mixture with whisked egg white folded in. As the soufflé cooks, the air expands, making the soufflé rise. Soufflé mixtures are usually based on a thick white sauce called a panada (or panade) to which egg yolks and flavourings are added.

Cheese Soufflé

SERVES 4

295 CALORIES/SERVING

15 ml (1 level tbsp) freshly grated Parmesan cheese
200 ml (7 fl oz) milk
few onion and carrot slices
1 bay leaf
6 black peppercorns
25 g (1 oz) butter or margarine
30 ml (2 level tbsp) white plain flour
10 ml (2 level tsp) Dijon mustard
salt and pepper
cayenne
4 eggs, separated, plus 1 egg white
75 g (3 oz) mature Cheddar cheese, finely grated

1 Grease a 1.3 litre (2 ¼ pint) soufflé dish with butter. Sprinkle the Parmesan into the dish and tilt the dish, knocking the sides gently until they are evenly coated with cheese. Put the milk in a saucepan with the onion and carrot slices, bay leaf and peppercorns. Bring slowly to the boil, then remove from the heat, cover and leave to infuse for 30 minutes. Strain.

2 Melt the butter in a saucepan and stir in the flour and mustard. Season with salt, pepper and cayenne, and cook for 1 minute, stirring. Remove from the heat and gradually stir in the milk. Bring to the boil slowly and cook, stirring, until the sauce thickens. Leave to cool a little, then beat in the egg yolks, one at a time. Reserve 15 ml (1 level tbsp) grated Cheddar, and stir the remainder into the sauce until evenly blended.

3 Using a hand or electric mixer, whisk the egg whites until they stand in soft peaks.

VARIATIONS

Replace the Cheddar cheese with one of the following:

Blue Cheese
Use a semi-hard blue cheese, such as Stilton or Wensleydale.

Mushroom
Add 125 g (4 oz) mushrooms, chopped and sautéed in butter.

Smoked Haddock
Add 75 g (3 oz) finely flaked cooked smoked haddock.

4 Mix one large spoonful of egg white into the sauce to lighten it. Gently pour the sauce over the remaining egg whites and carefully fold the ingredients together, using a metal spoon. Do not overmix.

5 Pour the soufflé mixture gently into the prepared dish; it should come about three-quarters of the way up the side of the dish.

6 Sprinkle with the reserved cheese and run a knife around the edge of the mixture. Stand the dish on a baking sheet and bake in the oven at 180°C (350°F) mark 4 for about 30 minutes or until golden brown on the top, well risen and just firm to the touch. Serve immediately. There should be a hint of softness in the centre of the soufflé.

Watchpoints

- Ideally, whisk the egg whites in a metal bowl; copper is best but stainless steel is also good. If beating by hand, use a balloon or rotary whisk or hand-held electric beater.

- Make sure the bowl and whisk are spotlessly clean. If there is any grease, the egg whites will not whisk to maximum volume.
- Use a proper straight-sided soufflé dish to get the best rise during cooking.

- Running a knife around the edge of the mixture before it goes into the oven helps to achieve the classic 'hat' effect.
- The weight of the flavouring ingredient should not be too great or the cooked soufflé will be heavy.

- The preparation of the panada is important, for unless it is smoothly blended and thoroughly amalgamated with the egg yolks, the cooked soufflé could have an unpleasant leathery texture.

Goat's Cheese Puffs

SERVES 6 AS A STARTER

125 CALORIES/PUFF

butter or margarine
15 ml (1 level tbsp) toasted hazelnuts, finely chopped
15 ml (1 level tbsp) fresh white breadcrumbs
15 ml (1 level tbsp) freshly grated Parmesan cheese
15 ml (1 level tbsp) plain white flour
75 ml (5 tbsp) semi-skimmed milk
1 egg yolk
125 g (4 oz) soft goat's cheese, crumbled
salt and pepper
4 egg whites
2.5 ml (½ tsp) lemon juice
oil
salad leaves, to serve

1 Grease and base-line eight 150 ml (¼ pint) ramekin dishes.
2 Mix the nuts with the breadcrumbs and Parmesan, and use to coat the insides of the ramekins, reserving some to sprinkle on the top.
3 Melt 15 g (½ oz) butter in a small saucepan. Add the flour and cook for 1 minute, stirring constantly. Remove from the heat and mix in the milk. Cook, stirring, over a moderate heat until the mixture forms a thick sauce. Cool slightly, then beat in the egg yolk and goat's cheese. Season with salt and pepper.
4 Whisk the egg whites with a pinch of salt and the lemon juice until they form stiff peaks. Using a large metal spoon, fold the cheese mixture into the egg whites.
5 Divide the mixture among the prepared dishes and top with the remaining crumb mixture. Place the ramekins in a roasting tin. Half-fill the tin with boiling water and bake in the oven at 190°C (375°F) mark 5 for 12–15 minutes.
6 Cool for 10 minutes, then turn out the puffs. Remove the lining paper and invert on to an oiled baking tray. Return to the oven or place under a hot grill to brown. Serve with salad leaves.

Spinach and Gruyère Soufflé

SERVES 3–4

520–400 CALORIES/SERVING

450 g (1 lb) spinach leaves, cooked, or 225 g (8 oz) frozen leaf spinach, thawed
50 g (2 oz) butter or margarine
45 ml (3 level tbsp) white plain flour
200 ml (7 fl oz) milk
salt and pepper
3 eggs, separated, plus 1 egg white
125 g (4 oz) Gruyère cheese, grated

1 Grease a 1.3 litre (2¼ pint) soufflé dish. Put the spinach in a sieve and press with the back of a spoon to remove all moisture. Chop finely.
2 Melt the butter in a saucepan, add the spinach and cook for a few minutes to drive off any moisture.
3 Add the flour and cook gently for 1 minute, stirring. Remove the pan from the heat and gradually stir in the milk. Season with salt and pepper and bring slowly to the boil. Reduce the heat and cook, stirring, until thickened. Cool slightly, then beat in the egg yolks, one at a time, and 75 g (3 oz) grated cheese.
4 Whisk the egg whites until stiff, then fold carefully into the mixture. Spoon into the prepared soufflé dish and sprinkle with the remaining cheese.
5 Stand the dish on a baking sheet and bake in the oven at 190°C (375°F) mark 5 for about 30 minutes or until well risen and just set. Serve immediately.

Toasted Walnut, Bacon and Roquefort Roulade

A roulade is made from a soufflé mixture baked in a lined Swiss roll tin, then turned out and rolled up with a hot filling inside.

SERVES 4–6

575–380 CALORIES/SERVING

6 lean streaky bacon rashers, derinded
25 g (1 oz) butter or margarine
25 g (1 oz) white plain flour
300 ml (½ pint) milk
50 g (2 oz) Roquefort cheese, crumbled
75 g (3 oz) walnut halves, toasted and roughly chopped
salt and pepper
700 g (1½ lb) fresh spinach, stalks removed, or 300 g (10 oz) packet frozen chopped spinach, thawed
1 garlic clove, crushed
45 ml (3 level tbsp) freshly grated Parmesan cheese
freshly grated nutmeg
4 eggs, separated
shavings of fresh Parmesan cheese and finely chopped toasted walnuts, to garnish

1 Grease a 33 × 23 cm (13 × 9 inch) Swiss roll tin and line with non-stick baking parchment. Grill the bacon until crisp, then chop into large pieces.

2 To make the filling, melt the butter in a saucepan, stir in the flour and cook for 1 minute. Remove from the heat and gradually stir in the milk. Return to the heat and bring to the boil, stirring continuously. Cook, stirring, for 2–3 minutes.

3 Remove from the heat and stir in the Roquefort cheese until melted. Add the bacon and walnuts, and season with pepper. Cover the surface with a piece of damp greaseproof paper to prevent a skin forming.

4 To make the roulade, put the fresh spinach in a saucepan with just the water clinging to the leaves after washing, cover tightly and cook for 4–5 minutes or until wilted. Drain well and chop very finely. If using frozen spinach, drain thoroughly.

5 Put the spinach in a bowl with the garlic and 30 ml (2 level tbsp) of the Parmesan. Stir well, seasoning with salt, pepper and plenty of nutmeg. Beat in the egg yolks.

6 Whisk the egg whites until stiff, and fold carefully into the spinach mixture. Pour into the prepared tin, then quickly spread out evenly. Bake in the oven at 200°C (400°F) mark 6 for about 15 minutes or until well risen and firm to the touch.

7 While the roulade is in the oven, spread out a sheet of non-stick baking parchment on the work surface and sprinkle with the remaining Parmesan. Reheat the filling when the roulade is almost cooked (it should be piping hot when spread on the roulade).

8 Turn the roulade out on to the sheet of paper and peel away the lining paper. Quickly spread with the hot filling. Roll up the roulade, gently lifting the paper. Transfer to a heated serving dish and sprinkle with shavings of Parmesan and a few chopped walnuts. Serve immediately.

Pancakes

Sweet or savoury, pancakes, or crêpes, are surprisingly versatile and convenient. They can be made ahead, and either kept in the refrigerator for 3–4 days or frozen, ready to reheat. Pancakes should be as thin as possible, almost lacy. This depends on the consistency of the batter and on using a good pan. The recipe opposite should make 12 pancakes, 16 if you're an expert or 8 if you're learning! There will always be a few disasters at first.

Basic Pancakes

MAKES ABOUT 12

70 CALORIES/PANCAKE (WITHOUT SUGAR)

200 ml (7 fl oz) milk
75 g (3 oz) white plain flour
pinch of salt
1 whole egg
1 egg yolk
15 ml (1 tbsp) vegetable oil
butter or vegetable oil for cooking
caster sugar and lemon juice, to serve

VARIATIONS

Cinnamon Pancakes
Add 2.5 ml (½ level tsp) ground cinnamon and 15 ml (1 level tbsp) caster sugar to the flour in step 1.

Lime Pancakes
Add the grated rind of 1 lime during step 1.

Buckwheat Pancakes
Use a mixture of half white and half buckwheat flour. Do not sift the buckwheat flour.

LEFT: *Chicken and Mushroom Pancakes (page 60)*

1 Make the milk up to 300 ml (½ pint) with water. Sift the flour and salt into a mixing bowl and make a well in the centre. Add the whole egg, the egg yolk and half the milk mixture to the well. With a wooden spoon or balloon whisk, gradually lap the flour into the liquid, beating until smooth. Stir in the remaining milk with 15 ml (1 tbsp) oil. Cover and leave in a cool place for about 1 hour.

2 Give the batter another whisk and pour into a measuring jug. Place a little butter or oil in a 15 cm (6 inch) base measurement pancake pan (see Cook's tip) and heat until very hot. Pour off excess fat, then pour a little batter into the pan, tilting the pan as you add the liquid so that it runs over the base of the pan in a thin, even layer. Quickly pour excess batter back into the jug. (You'll now have a lip of batter up the side of the pan. Cut and remove this with a palette knife to neaten the shape.)

3 Place the pan over a moderate heat and cook for 30 seconds– 1 minute or until the pancake browns around the edges and begins to curl away from the pan. Slide a flexible palette knife under the pancake (a fish slice is too rigid) and flip it over. (If your fingers are quite heat-resistant, you can turn the pancake with your hands.) Brown the underside of the pancake for about 30 seconds.

4 Turn the pancake out on to a wire rack lined with a tea towel. Fold the towel over the pancake to keep it moist. Continue to make about 12 pancakes in all, stacking them with pieces of greaseproof paper between them. If the pancakes start to stick when cooking, add a little more butter or oil to the pan. Divide the pancakes into two stacks and wrap in foil. Reheat in the oven at 190°C (375°F) mark 5 for 8–10 minutes. Fold into fan shapes and serve with a little caster sugar and lemon juice.

Watchpoints
• Ensure that the batter is quite smooth before adding the remaining milk mixture. It can be made in a food processor. Blend the flour, salt, egg, egg yolk and half the milk mixture until smooth, then add the remaining ingredients and blend again quickly until smooth. Do not overbeat as this will produce tough pancakes.
• Use the minimum amount of butter or oil; the pan should be almost dry.
• If the pan is not really hot before cooking the batter, the pancakes will be leathery.
• Keep pancakes covered to prevent them drying out while cooking the remainder.

Cook's tip
A good, heavy-based pan is essential for pancake making. A new pan should be 'seasoned' before using. Leave it to soak with oil and salt for several hours. Heat the oil to a high temperature and pour off, then wipe out the pan with absorbent kitchen paper. Non-stick pans do not require seasoning.

Freezer notes
To freeze: Wrap and freeze after frying but before reheating.
To use: Thaw at cool room temperature for about 4 hours, then reheat as in step 4.

Smoked Haddock and Egg Pancakes

SERVES 3–4

720–540 CALORIES/SERVING

350 g (12 oz) smoked haddock fillet
2 eggs
40 g (1½ oz) butter or margarine
25 g (1 oz) white plain flour
200 ml (7 fl oz) milk
150 ml (¼ pint) soured cream
15 ml (1 level tbsp) snipped fresh chives
pepper
6 Basic Pancakes (see page 59)
50 g (2 oz) fresh brown breadcrumbs

1 Poach the fish in enough water to cover for about 5–7 minutes or until tender. Drain, skin and flake into large pieces, removing any bones. Hard-boil the eggs for 7 minutes, then shell and chop them roughly.

2 Melt 25 g (1 oz) butter in a saucepan, add the flour and cook, stirring, for 1 minute. Remove from the heat and gradually stir in the milk and soured cream. Bring to the boil, stirring constantly, then lower the heat and cook gently, stirring, for 2–3 minutes.

3 Add the flaked fish and roughly chopped eggs to the sauce. Stir in the chives and season with plenty of pepper; the fish adds sufficient salt. Divide the mixture among the prepared pancakes and roll up.

4 Place the pancakes in a shallow ovenproof dish and sprinkle with the breadcrumbs. Melt the remaining butter and drizzle over the top. Bake in the oven at 190°C (375°F) mark 5 for about 20 minutes or until bubbling and thoroughly heated through.

Smoked Haddock and Egg Pancakes

Chicken and Mushroom Pancakes

SERVES 6

460 CALORIES/SERVING

50 g (2 oz) butter or margarine
225 g (8 oz) button mushrooms, wiped and sliced
25 g (1 oz) white plain flour
300 ml (½ pint) chicken stock
350 g (12 oz) cooked chicken, roughly shredded
salt and pepper
12 Buckwheat Pancakes (see page 59)
125 g (4 oz) Gruyère cheese, grated

1 Melt the butter in a saucepan, add the mushrooms and cook for 2–3 minutes. Stir in the flour and cook, stirring, for 1 minute, then stir in the stock. Bring to the boil, stirring, then simmer for 2–3 minutes. Stir in the chicken, and season with salt and pepper.

2 Spoon some of the chicken and mushroom mixture on to a quarter of each pancake. Fold in half, and then in half again to form neat pockets. Arrange in a lightly greased ovenproof dish.

3 Sprinkle liberally with the grated cheese and bake in the oven at 190°C (375°F) mark 5 for 25 minutes or until golden and bubbly.

Apple and Cinnamon Pancakes with Mascarpone Cream

SERVES 8

340 CALORIES/SERVING

125 g (4 oz) mascarpone cheese (see Cook's tip)
150 ml (5 fl oz) Greek natural yogurt
icing sugar
900 g (2 lb) cooking apples
75 g (3 oz) butter
50 g (2 oz) soft light brown sugar
15 ml (1 tbsp) lemon juice
75 g (3 oz) seedless raisins
90 ml (6 tbsp) maple-flavoured sauce
8 Cinnamon Pancakes (see page 59)
ground mixed spice, to dust

1 To make the mascarpone cream, mix together the mascarpone cheese, yogurt and about 15 ml (1 level tbsp) icing sugar, or to taste. Cover and chill.

2 Peel, quarter, core and thickly slice the apples. Melt 50 g (2 oz) butter in a saucepan and add the apples, brown sugar and lemon juice. Cover tightly and cook gently for about 10 minutes or until the apples are beginning to soften but still retain some shape. Stir in the raisins and 60 ml (4 tbsp) maple-flavoured sauce. Leave to cool.

3 Lightly butter an ovenproof dish. Divide the apple mixture among the pancakes and roll up. Arrange in the dish. Melt the remaining butter and mix with the remaining 30 ml (2 tbsp) maple-flavoured sauce. Drizzle over the pancakes and cover tightly with foil.

4 Bake in the oven at 190°C (375°F) mark 5 for about 20 minutes or until piping hot. Serve with the mascarpone cream, dusted with mixed spice.

Cook's tip

Mascarpone cheese is a high-fat soft cheese sold in delicatessens and supermarkets. Alternatively, use a full-fat soft cheese.

Souffléd Lime Pancakes

SERVES 6

350 CALORIES/SERVING

4 limes
1 lemon
175 g (6 oz) caster sugar
225 ml (8 fl oz) milk
50 g (2 oz) butter
40 g (1½ oz) white plain flour
3 whole eggs, separated, plus 1 egg yolk
6 Lime Pancakes (see page 59)
icing sugar, to dust
mint sprigs, to decorate

1 To make the caramel sauce, pare the rind from one lime and the lemon, and slice the fruit. In a small saucepan, dissolve 125 g (4 oz) sugar in 150 ml (¼ pint) water. Bring to the boil and bubble to a golden caramel. Take off the heat and pour in 75 ml (3 fl oz) warm water. Add the pared rind, and simmer for 1–2 minutes or until the caramel is smooth. Leave to cool. Stir in the sliced fruit with 15 ml (1 tbsp) lime juice.

2 To make the soufflé, bring the milk to the boil and, in a separate saucepan, melt the butter. Stir the flour into the butter, then remove from the heat and gradually stir in the boiling milk. Add the grated rind and juice of the remaining two limes with the remaining caster sugar. Bring to the boil, stirring, then simmer for 1 minute.

3 Off the heat, beat in the four egg yolks, then stir over a low heat for 2–3 minutes. Spoon into a bowl, cover the surface with damp greaseproof paper and leave to cool for about 20 minutes.

4 Whisk the three egg whites until they stand in soft peaks. Beat the egg yolk mixture until smooth. Stir one large spoonful of egg white into the sauce to lighten it, then gently fold in the remainder.

5 Thoroughly grease a baking sheet. Place one pancake on the baking sheet and spoon one sixth of the soufflé mixture on to one half of the pancake. Fold over to enclose. Repeat with the remaining pancakes. Dust lightly with icing sugar.

6 Bake in the oven at 220°C (425°F) mark 7 for 10–12 minutes or until lightly set. Decorate with mint sprigs and serve immediately with the caramel sauce.

Meringue

Meringue is made from a mixture of whisked egg white and sugar, which is very slowly baked in the oven so it dries out and becomes crisp and firm. The light texture is the perfect foil for creamy fillings and soft fruit. Making simple meringue, sometimes called Swiss meringue, is easy if you follow the basic rules.

Basic Meringue

MAKES ABOUT 20 FILLED MERINGUES

110 CALORIES/FILLED MERINGUE

4 egg whites (size 2)

225 g (8 oz) caster sugar

284 ml (10 fl oz) carton double cream, to fill

icing sugar, to dust

grated chocolate, to decorate

VARIATION

Brown Sugar Meringue
Simply replace half the sugar with soft light brown sugar.

1 Place the egg whites in a large, clean, dry, grease-free bowl. Whisk the egg whites until they stand in stiff peaks, continually moving the whisk around the bowl to ensure they are all evenly whisked. To test the consistency, lift the whisk out of the bowl: the egg white sticking to it should stand in stiff peaks that do not fall over at the tip.

2 Whisk in half the caster sugar, adding 25 g (1 oz) at a time, whisking between each addition until the mixture becomes stiff and satiny-looking. The peaks of meringue should now just flop over at the tip. Sprinkle the remaining caster sugar over the egg whites and use a large metal spoon or plastic spatula to fold it in lightly. Do not use a wooden spoon to fold in the sugar as its thick, blunt edge will knock all the air out of the meringue.

3 To pipe the meringues, fit a large piping bag with a 1 cm (½ inch) plain nozzle, keeping the seam of the bag on the outside. Hold the bag in one hand and fold back a cuff of material over your knuckles. Half-fill the bag with meringue, pull up the cuff and twist the top to prevent the meringue from oozing out. Hold the bag in one hand vertically above a baking sheet lined with non-stick baking parchment. Support the base with your other hand. Pipe whatever shapes you need by gently squeezing the end of the bag. To finish, ease the pressure and lift off the bag. Make sure the meringues have room to spread.

4 Bake in the oven at 100°C (200°F) mark low for about 2 hours or until dried out. Swap the baking sheets around to ensure even drying. When dry, the meringues should be crisp and pale golden, and should peel cleanly off the paper. Cool on wire racks, then store in airtight containers for up to 2 months. To fill the meringues, whip the double cream and sandwich between two meringues. Dust with icing sugar and decorate with grated chocolate. Refrigerate: left for 1 hour they will still be crisp, after 2 hours they will become chewy, after 3 hours they will go soggy.

*Meringues with Grand Marnier
and Chocolate Sauce (page 64)*

Watchpoints
• Make sure all equipment is scrupulously clean and dry; egg white hates grease and moisture and won't whisk properly if there are any traces.
• The egg whites and yolks must be carefully separated; break each white into a bowl before adding it to the others, in case any yolk escapes.
• For maximum volume, leave whites at cool room temperature for 2 hours before using. They should be whisked until they form stiff peaks – any further and water will seep out of the egg whites, leaving the whites too dry so that they lose bulk, as they do if left to stand after whisking.

Freezer notes
To freeze: Pack unfilled in rigid containers and freeze.
To use: Thaw at cool room temperature for 1 hour.

What went wrong?
Most problems with meringue can be prevented. These tips will help you avoid the most common pitfalls.

Piped meringue won't keep its shape because mixture is too runny.
Egg yolk or grease on whisk or bowl, or the egg whites were not whisked enough in step 1, or the first quantity of sugar was insufficiently whisked in.

An uneven surface, tiny cracks and large air holes.
Overwhisked egg whites.

Smooth outside with a hard, close texture and very soft and chewy inside, or sugar has bubbled out.
Sugar added too quickly or too much at once. If sugar weeps from cracks, turn meringue over on to a clean sheet of non-stick baking parchment and return it to the oven to dry out.

Meringue is overcooked.
Break it up roughly, fold into whipped double cream and a thick fruit purée and freeze. Serve as a frozen dessert.

Hazelnut and Chocolate Meringue Cake

SERVES 10

430 CALORIES/SERVING

175 g (6 oz) hazelnuts

1 quantity Brown Sugar Meringue (see page 62)

125 g (4 oz) plain chocolate

450 ml (15 fl oz) double cream

icing sugar, to dust

1 Toast the hazelnuts until well browned, then rub off the skins and leave to cool. Finely chop 125 g (4 oz) toasted hazelnuts and grind the remainder. Line two baking sheets with non-stick baking parchment and draw a 20.5 cm (8 inch) circle on each. Turn the paper over so the pencil marks are underneath.

2 Prepare Brown Sugar Meringue as far as step 2 of Basic Meringue, folding in three-quarters of the chopped hazelnuts with the sugar.

3 Spread the meringue mixture in the rounds marked on the baking parchment, using the pencil marks as a guide. Sprinkle the remaining chopped nuts over one meringue round.

4 Bake in the oven at 150°C (300°F) mark 2 for about 1½ hours or until the meringue is well dried out. Remove from the oven and leave to cool. When quite cold, peel off the non-stick paper.

5 Meanwhile, prepare the chocolate ganache. Break up the chocolate and place it in a small saucepan with 150 ml (5 fl oz) cream. Warm gently until the chocolate melts, stirring occasionally. Bring to the boil, stirring, then remove from the heat and stir in the ground hazelnuts. Cool, cover and refrigerate until required. Allow the mixture to soften at room temperature for about 1 hour before using.

6 Carefully spread the softened chocolate mixture over the plain meringue round. Whip the remaining cream and spread over the chocolate. Top with the nut-topped meringue round. Refrigerate for 2–3 hours before serving, dusted with icing sugar.

Hazelnut and Chocolate Meringue Cake

Meringues with Grand Marnier and Chocolate Sauce

SERVES 8

485 CALORIES/SERVING

For the meringues

4 egg whites (size 2)

225 g (8 oz) caster sugar

For the filling and sauce

150 g (5 oz) sultanas, roughly chopped

45 ml (3 tbsp) Grand Marnier or Cointreau

284 ml (10 fl oz) carton double cream

200 g (7 oz) plain chocolate

icing sugar, for dusting

1 Soak the sultanas in the Grand Marnier for 4 hours.

2 Meanwhile, make the meringues following steps 1–4 of Basic Meringue (see page 62), piping the mixture in about 32 ovals on to the lined baking sheets.

3 About 2 hours before serving, whip all but 45 ml (3 tbsp) of the cream, then fold in the sultanas and Grand Marnier. Sandwich the meringues with the cream and pile into a dish. Grate over a little chocolate and dust with icing sugar. Cover and chill until required.

4 To make the sauce, break the remaining chocolate into a saucepan and add the remaining cream and 150 ml (¼ pint) water. Warm gently until the chocolate melts, stirring occasionally. Simmer gently for about 3 minutes, stirring frequently, until slightly thickened.

Iced Maple and Ginger Meringue Cake

SERVES 8

385 CALORIES/SERVING

175 g (6 oz) mixed walnuts and hazelnuts
5 egg whites
275 g (10 oz) caster sugar
50 g (2 oz) stem ginger
3 whole eggs
60 ml (4 tbsp) maple-flavoured syrup
300 ml (½ pint) Greek natural yogurt
kumquats, walnuts and icing sugar, to decorate

1 Draw two 20.5 cm (8 inch) circles on non-stick baking parchment. Turn the paper over and place on baking sheets. Brown the nuts under the grill, allow to cool, then roughly chop.
2 Whisk the egg whites with an electric whisk until stiff but not dry. Gradually add half the caster sugar, whisking after each addition, until the meringue is stiff and glossy. Fold in the remaining sugar and half the nuts.
3 Spread half the meringue on one paper circle, and the remainder in irregular shapes on the second circle.
4 Bake in the oven at 110°C (225°F) mark ¼ for about 2½ hours. (The meringue will weep.) Turn off the oven and allow to cool completely. Peel off the paper.
5 Chop the stem ginger. Separate the whole eggs and whisk the yolks and maple-flavoured syrup until thick and mousse-like. Fold in the yogurt with the ginger, remaining nuts and the whisked egg whites. Freeze for 2–2½ hours, stirring about every 30 minutes, until the ice is thick enough to sandwich between the meringues.
6 Spread the ice mixture on to the smooth meringue circle and place the irregular one on the top. Freeze for at least 4 hours or until firm.
7 Place in the refrigerator for 1½ hours before slicing. Decorate with kumquats, walnuts and icing sugar.

Lemon and Lime Meringue Pie

SERVES 8

400 CALORIES/SERVING

150 g (5 oz) butter
175 g (6 oz) white plain flour
125 g (4 oz) caster sugar
3 egg yolks
finely grated rind and juice of 1 large lemon
finely grated rind and juice of 2 limes
75 ml (5 level tbsp) cornflour
Basic Meringue made using 3 egg whites and 175 g (6 oz) caster sugar (see page 62)
lemon and lime slices, to decorate
icing sugar, to dust (optional)
single cream, to accompany

1 Rub 125 g (4 oz) butter into the flour until the mixture resembles fine breadcrumbs. Add 25 g (1 oz) caster sugar. Beat 1 egg yolk with 15–30 ml (1–2 tbsp) water, and use to bind the mixture to a firm dough. Knead lightly, then roll out and use to line a 23 cm (9 inch) base measurement fluted flan tin. Prick the base of the pastry with a fork and line with greaseproof paper or foil. Fill with baking beans and bake blind in the oven at 200°C (400°F) mark 6 for 12–15 minutes or until set and lightly browned.
2 Meanwhile, prepare the filling. Place the lemon and lime rinds in a saucepan with 45 ml (3 tbsp) lemon juice and all the lime juice. Add 300 ml (½ pint) water and the remaining 75 g (3 oz) sugar, and warm gently until the sugar dissolves.
3 Mix the cornflour to a smooth paste with 90 ml (6 tbsp) water. Off the heat, stir the cornflour paste into the warm juices, then bring to the boil, stirring all the time. Cook for 1–2 minutes. Cool slightly, then beat in the remaining 2 egg yolks and 25 g (1 oz) butter. Pour into the prepared flan case.
4 Prepare the meringue to the end of step 2 of Basic Meringue. Spoon it over the lemon and lime filling to cover completely. Rough up the surface of the meringue with a blunt knife or a fork.
5 Bake in the oven at 150°C (300°F) mark 2 for about 35 minutes. The meringue will be soft inside. Cool for 20 minutes, then decorate with lemon and lime slices and dust with icing sugar, if wished. Serve warm, with cream.

FISH AND SHELLFISH

As the range and choice of available fish grows, so its popularity increases. It is now recognised as a useful and nutritious ingredient that should not be neglected. This chapter concentrates on techniques that make the most of the huge range of fish and shellfish available rather than on the fish themselves. It features poached whole salmon, grilled monkfish, rolled plaice fillets and scallops. Other fish can, of course, be substituted for those used in the recipes on the following pages. Most fishmongers, if asked, will prepare fresh fish for you, but the techniques described include filleting flat fish, cleaning mussels and opening scallops. These are not difficult to carry out at home and will become less time-consuming as you become more practised. A whole poached salmon makes an impressive buffet-table centrepiece but might seem too daunting a task to attempt. The instructions, photographs and watchpoints given, however, show it to be the simple technique it really is.

Poached Salmon

Poaching is a gentle method of cooking that keeps the flesh of fish moist. The salmon is placed in a fish kettle or large roasting tin and covered with liquid, which is slowly brought to the boil, simmered for 2 minutes only and allowed to cool down again. This may sound unbelievable, but it does work. The larger the fish, the more water it takes to cover it, and so the longer it takes to come up to the boil and cool down.

Dill-glazed Salmon

SERVES 8–10

450 CALORIES/SERVING FOR 8

1.8–2 kg (4–4½ lb) salmon or sea trout, cleaned

about 150 ml (¼ pint) dry white wine

slices of carrot, onion and celery for flavouring

2 bay leaves

few black peppercorns

large bunch of dill

lemon slices

salt and pepper

5 ml (1 level tsp) powdered gelatine

salad leaves, to garnish

Mayonnaise, made with lemon juice (see page 10), to accompany

1 Rinse the salmon under cold running water. Cut off the head, if wished, and snip the tail into a V-shape. Place the salmon on the strainer in an 18 × 60 cm (7 × 24 inch) fish kettle or in a roasting tin (see note). Pour over just enough water to cover, with the white wine. Add the sliced vegetables, the bay leaves, black peppercorns, dill stalks, lemon slices and seasoning. Refrigerate the remaining dill.

2 Cover the fish kettle and bring the liquid slowly to the boil. (This will take about 15 minutes.) Simmer for 2 minutes only. Take the fish kettle off the heat and leave the salmon in the liquid until cold, without taking the lid off. (This can take as long as 1 hour.) Once cold, lift the strainer and salmon out of the fish kettle and drain for a few minutes.

3 Strain off and reserve the poaching liquor. Using your hands to lift the fish, carefully place it on a large board, flat side uppermost. Using a sharp knife, peel away the skin. For a buffet, a salmon looks better with head and tail intact, so unless it really worries you, leave them on. Ease out the fin bones, and scrape away the brownish flesh, leaving the pink flesh below.

4 Turn the fish over and place on a board or flat platter. Carefully peel away the skin and scrape away the brownish flesh, as before. Don't worry if any cracks appear, as the dill glaze will cover them. Cover and refrigerate.

5 For the glaze, pour 200 ml (7 fl oz) of the reserved cooking liquor through a sieve lined with muslin into a small heatproof bowl. Sprinkle over the gelatine and leave to soak for about 10 minutes. Dissolve the gelatine by standing the bowl in a saucepan of simmering water until it liquefies.

6 Stand the bowl in a pan of iced water and stir until the liquid cools and begins to thicken. Brush a little glaze over the fish and press tiny dill sprigs into it. Chill for 10 minutes. Spoon over the remaining glaze and refrigerate. Using fish slices, lift the salmon on to a serving platter. Garnish with salad leaves and serve with the lemon mayonnaise.

Freezer notes

To freeze: Overwrap and freeze at the end of step 4. Pack and freeze the liquor separately.
To use: Thaw overnight at cool room temperature, then complete as in the recipe.

To Poach in a Roasting Tin

1 Line a large, deep roasting tin with foil (a 30.5 × 38 cm/12 × 15 inch tin is ideal). Curl the prepared fish into the roasting tin. Pour over enough water to fill the tin by three-quarters, adding wine and flavourings, as in Dill-glazed Salmon. Cover the tin tightly with foil.

2 Place on the hob and bring slowly to the boil. Simmer for 5 minutes only. Remove from the heat, leave covered, and allow to go quite cold. Alternatively, cook in the oven at 180°C (350°F) mark 4 for about 1 hour. Leave covered, and allow to go quite cold.

3 Finish as for Dill-glazed Salmon, using the foil to help lift the fish out of the roasting tin.

Watchpoints

• Rinse fish well to ensure all traces of blood are removed.

• Bring slowly to the boil to prevent the fish from breaking up in the kettle.

• Leave to cool completely before uncovering the fish. Don't be tempted to lift the lid or heat will escape and the fish may not cook through.

• If the salmon breaks up at all, don't worry – just patch the flesh neatly together on the serving plate. All our dressings and serving ideas are designed to camouflage any unwanted cracks!

• Ease the skin away gently, taking care not to pull away any flesh from the fish.

• Dissolve the gelatine over a gentle heat – if you boil it, it won't set.

• If the glaze sets before you've brushed it over the fish, warm gently to dissolve it again.

Celebration Salmon

This makes the ideal buffet dish as the boned fish is so easy to serve. After filleting the fish, always check for any stray bones by running your fingers along the flesh. We've allowed plenty of stuffing so that there is a generous layer between the fish fillets.

SERVES 10–12

670 CALORIES/SERVING FOR **10**

5 ml (1 level tsp) saffron strands
bunch of watercress
300 ml (½ pint) Mayonnaise, made with lemon juice (see page 10)
45 ml (3 tbsp) single cream
salt and pepper
125 g (4 oz) long grain and wild rice mixed
½ medium cucumber
125 g (4 oz) smoked salmon trimmings
125 g (4 oz) cooked peeled prawns
lemon juice, to taste
1.8–2 kg (4–4½ lb) salmon or sea trout, cooked and prepared as in steps 1–4 of Dill-glazed Salmon (see page 68)
125 g (4 oz) large smoked salmon slices
lemon and cucumber slices and watercress sprigs, to garnish

1 Prepare the saffron mayonnaise. Cover the saffron with 15 ml (1 tbsp) boiling water and leave to stand for 15 minutes. Strain and keep the liquid. Place half the watercress in a food processor with the lemon mayonnaise and strained liquid. Blend until the watercress is finely chopped. Turn out into a bowl and stir in the cream. Season with salt and pepper.

2 Prepare the stuffing. Cook the rice in boiling salted water until tender, then drain well. Peel and dice the cucumber, put it in a colander and sprinkle with salt. Leave for 20 minutes, then rinse under cold running water and drain well. Finely chop the smoked salmon trimmings and the remaining watercress. Mix with the prawns and about 60 ml (4 level tbsp) of the saffron mayonnaise to bind. Season and add lemon juice to taste.

3 Using a small sharp knife, carefully cut down the central line of the flatter side of the salmon. Ease the top fillets away from the bone. Place these fillets together again, skin side down, on a serving dish. Spoon the stuffing over the fillets.

4 Lift and ease the bone off the remaining side of salmon. Run your fingers along the fillet to ensure all bones are removed. Turn over. Cover the salmon with the smoked salmon slices. Place the fillets on top of the stuffing.

5 Garnish with very thin cucumber and lemon slices and watercress. Cover and refrigerate. Serve accompanied by the mayonnaise.

Hot Salmon and Mushroom Crisp

SERVES 8

700 CALORIES/SERVING

45 ml (3 tbsp) olive oil

225 g (8 oz) mixed button and wild mushrooms, wiped and chopped

175 g (6 oz) bulb of Florence fennel, trimmed and roughly chopped

15 ml (3 level tsp) chopped fresh tarragon

salt and pepper

225 g (8 oz) puff pastry, thawed if frozen

1.6 kg (3½ lb) salmon or sea trout, cooked and prepared as in steps 1–4 of Dill-glazed Salmon (see page 68)

50 g (2 oz) butter, melted

about 150 g (5 oz) filo pastry

150 ml (¼ pint) white wine

142 ml (5 fl oz) carton double cream

1 Prepare the stuffing. Heat the oil in a large frying pan, add the mushrooms and fennel, and cook over a moderate heat for 4–5 minutes. Turn into a bowl. Stir in 5 ml (1 level tsp) tarragon and salt and pepper to taste. Cool, cover and chill until required.

2 Meanwhile, roll out the puff pastry to a rectangle measuring about 18 × 40.5 cm (7 × 16 inches). Place on a wet baking sheet and prick well with a fork. Bake in the oven at 200°C (400°F) mark 6 for 15 minutes. Cool.

3 Bone the salmon as in steps 3 and 4 of Celebration Salmon. Place one side of the salmon on the puff pastry. Spoon over the stuffing mixture and top with the remaining side of salmon. Trim any excess pastry to about 2.5 cm (1 inch) away from the edge of the fish.

4 Brush the exposed pastry edges with melted butter, then cover the fish with overlapping layers of filo pastry, brushing with butter. Tuck the edges underneath. Top with crumpled filo pastry, and brush with butter.

5 Bake the fish in the oven at 200°C (400°F) mark 6 for 35–40 minutes, covering loosely with foil.

6 Put 600 ml (1 pint) of the reserved poaching liquor in a saucepan with the wine, bring to the boil and boil until reduced to 300 ml (½ pint). Add the cream and simmer for 5 minutes to thicken. Add the remaining tarragon, simmer for 1–2 minutes, then season.

7 Serve the salmon warm, accompanied by the sauce.

Luxury Salmon Fishcakes

MAKES 16

185 CALORIES/FISHCAKE

350 g (12 oz) poached fresh salmon (see page 68), flaked

225 g (8 oz) smoked salmon, roughly chopped

350 g (12 oz) freshly cooked mashed potato

15 ml (1 tbsp) lemon juice

pepper

75 g (3 oz) butter, melted

45 ml (3 level tbsp) chopped fresh dill or 15 ml (1 level tbsp) dried dill weed

2 eggs, beaten

about 225 g (8 oz) dried white breadcrumbs

vegetable oil for frying

1 Mix the fresh and smoked salmon with the mashed potato, lemon juice, pepper to taste, butter and dill. Add just enough beaten egg to bind the mixture together. It should be firm, not sloppy. Cool, if necessary, then refrigerate for 1 hour or until very firm.

2 Shape the mixture into 16 cakes about 2.5 cm (1 inch) thick. Brush with some of the remaining beaten egg and coat with breadcrumbs. Chill for 30 minutes to firm.

3 Coat the cakes with egg and crumbs once more. Chill again until firm.

4 Heat some oil in a large frying pan and shallow-fry the fishcakes in batches for 3–4 minutes on each side, or until golden brown. Drain on absorbent kitchen paper and keep warm in the oven until all the fishcakes are cooked.

Cook's tips

• Cook the potato specially for the fishcakes; leftovers will be too stodgy. Invest in a gadget called a potato ricer which looks like a giant garlic press. It makes mashing potatoes easy – and no lumps!

• If dried white breadcrumbs are difficult to find, try using medium matzo meal.

Freezer notes

To freeze: Open freeze the fishcakes without egg and crumbs and pack into a rigid container, interleaving with non-stick paper.

To use: Thaw overnight in the refrigerator, coat with egg and crumbs and fry as in step 4.

Grilled Monkfish

Grilling is one of the quickest and simplest of cooking methods, and is ideal for fish. Whether grilling fish fillets, steaks or whole fish, the flesh will be succulent and tender. The firm flesh of white fish, such as monkfish, is well suited to grilling kebab-style, on skewers.

Seafood Kebabs

SERVES 4

130 CALORIES/SERVING

450 g (1 lb) monkfish or cod fillet

125 g (4 oz) cucumber

50 g (2 oz) large cooked prawns in shells

1 lime or lemon, thinly sliced

75 ml (3 fl oz) garlic vinaigrette

15 ml (1 level tbsp) chopped fresh dill or 2.5 ml (½ level tsp) dried dill weed

salt and pepper

salad leaves, to serve

dill sprigs, to garnish

Monkfish

Most good fishmongers and supermarkets stock monkfish nowadays, although it hasn't always been a popular fish because of its ugly appearance when whole. For this reason, it is almost always displayed without the head, which is its ugliest part, and many fishmongers also skin and fillet it before offering it for sale. Monkfish fillets and steaks taste very like lobster and scampi, however, at a fraction of the price!

Garlic Vinaigrette

For a simple vinaigrette, put 75 ml (3 fl oz) olive oil in a screw-topped jar with 30 ml (2 tbsp) white wine vinegar, a pinch of caster sugar, 5 ml (1 level tsp) Dijon mustard and 1 crushed garlic clove. Season with salt and pepper and shake well to mix.

Watchpoints
• Baste and turn the kebabs frequently during cooking to keep the fish moist and prevent the surface drying out.
• Keep the grill at a moderate heat only to avoid overcooking.

1 Skin the fish, if necessary, then cut into 2.5 cm (1 inch) cubes. Halve the cucumber lengthways and slice thickly.

2 Peel the prawns, leaving the tail shells on.

3 Thread the prawns and lime slices on to four wooden skewers, alternating with the cubes of fish and cucumber. Place the kebabs in a flameproof dish.

4 Spoon the vinaigrette and dill over the kebabs. Grill for 8–10 minutes, turning and basting occasionally. Season with salt and pepper, and serve immediately on a bed of salad leaves. Garnish with dill.

3 Thread the fish, onion pieces, aubergines and lemon slices alternately on to eight wooden skewers. Place the kebabs side by side in a non-metallic dish.
4 Whisk together the lemon juice, honey, soy sauce and tomato purée. Season with salt and pepper, and spoon over the kebabs. Cover and leave to marinate in the refrigerator for at least 12 hours, turning once.
5 Place the kebabs in a grill pan. Brush with a little of the marinade and grill for 10–12 minutes, turning occasionally, until all the ingredients are tender. Serve the kebabs garnished with frisée.

Grilled Monkfish with Lemon and Dill

SERVES 4

200 CALORIES/SERVING

700 g (1½ lb) monkfish tail, or other firm white fish

45 ml (3 tbsp) lemon juice

15 ml (1 level tbsp) chopped fresh dill or 2.5 ml (½ level tsp) dried dill weed

2 garlic cloves, sliced

45 ml (3 tbsp) olive oil

salt and pepper

lemon slices, to garnish

1 Remove all membrane from the fish and cut out the backbone to give two long fillets. Cut these in half to give four 'steaks'. Place in a non-metallic dish.
2 Whisk the lemon juice with the dill, garlic and olive oil. Season well with salt and pepper. Pour over the fish, cover and leave in a cool place to marinate for at least 4 hours, turning occasionally.
3 Drain the fish, arrange on a wire rack in a grill pan and grill for about 6 minutes on each side, basting regularly with the marinade. Serve immediately, garnished with lemon slices.

Sweet and Sour Monkfish Kebabs

SERVES 4

355 CALORIES/SERVING

450 g (1 lb) monkfish fillet, skinned

12 streaky bacon rashers, derinded

1 small aubergine, about 125 g (4 oz), thinly sliced

2 small red onions, peeled

2 lemons or limes, sliced

15 ml (1 tbsp) lemon juice

30 ml (2 tbsp) clear honey

15 ml (1 tbsp) soy sauce

15 ml (1 tbsp) tomato purée

salt and pepper

frisée, to garnish

1 Cut the monkfish into 2.5 cm (1 inch) cubes. Stretch the bacon rashers with the back of a knife and cut in half. Wrap a piece of bacon around each fish cube.
2 Blanch the aubergine slices in boiling water, drain and dry on absorbent kitchen paper. Quarter the onions, then separate each quarter into two, to give thinner pieces.

Grilled Monkfish with Lemon and Dill

10 minutes, turning frequently during cooking and brushing with the parsley mixture with each turn.

4 Arrange the hot skewers on a serving platter lined with shredded lettuce. Garnish with lemon slices and serve immediately.

Cook's tip

To prepare fresh mussels in the shell, put them in the sink and, under cold running water, scrape off any mud or barnacles with a small sharp knife. Pull away the hair-like 'beard' that protrudes from the shell. Tap any mussels that remain open with the back of the knife. If they refuse to close, throw them away. Rinse again in cold water until there is no trace of sand. To cook the mussels, place them in a large saucepan containing 1 cm (½ inch) boiling water. Cover and cook over a high heat for about 5 minutes or until the shells open, shaking the pan frequently. Discard any mussels that do not open. When cool enough to handle, remove the mussels from their shells with a small sharp knife.

Monkfish and Mussel Skewers

SERVES 4

415 CALORIES/SERVING

12 streaky bacon rashers, derinded
700 g (1½ lb) monkfish fillet, skinned
24 mussels, cooked and shelled (see Cook's tip)
25 g (1 oz) butter or margarine
60 ml (4 level tbsp) chopped fresh parsley
finely grated rind and juice of 1 large lemon
4 garlic cloves, crushed
pepper
shredded lettuce, to serve
lemon slices, to garnish

1 Halve the bacon rashers and roll up neatly. Cut the monkfish into 2.5 cm (1 inch) cubes. Thread the cubed fish, mussels and bacon alternately on to 12 oiled skewers.

2 Melt the butter in a saucepan, then remove from the heat and add the parsley, lemon rind and juice, and garlic. Season with pepper; the mussels and bacon should provide sufficient salt.

3 Place the skewers on an oiled grill rack and brush with the parsley mixture. Cook under a moderate grill for

Plaice Rolls

Flat fish, such as plaice and sole, are very popular and easy to prepare once you have mastered the basic techniques. Fillets of flat fish can be used in a number of flavoursome and elegant dishes. You can, of course, buy fish ready-filleted from your fishmonger or supermarket, but it is easy to fillet flat fish at home following the steps below.

Rolled Plaice with Pesto

SERVES 4

225 CALORIES/SERVING

| 4 small whole plaice, skinned |
| 3 spring onions |
| 125 g (4 oz) fine asparagus or French beans |
| 1 carrot, peeled |
| 15 ml (1 tbsp) pesto |
| 30 ml (2 tbsp) lemon juice |
| 100 ml (4 fl oz) fish stock |
| salt and pepper |
| 75 g (3 oz) oyster or button mushrooms, wiped |
| 125 g (4 oz) baby corn cobs, halved |
| 125 g (4 oz) mangetouts |
| 30 ml (2 tbsp) oil (optional) |

1 Lay each fish in turn on a board with its tail pointing towards you and its eyes facing up. Cut down the centre of the fish from head to tail along the backbone.

2 Starting at the head end, insert the blade of the knife between the flesh and the bones. Aiming to skim the blade over the bones, cut down along the flesh. When the head end of the fillet is detached, lift it and continue cutting until the whole fillet is removed.

3 Repeat this procedure to remove the second fillet.

4 Turn the fish over and cut two more fillets from the other side. When all the fillets are removed you should be left with a clean skeleton and four neat fillets. Roll the fillets up loosely, skinned side in.

5 Cut the spring onions, asparagus and carrot into 6 cm (2½ inch) lengths.

6 Place the fish in a shallow pan. Mix the pesto with the lemon juice and stock, pour over the fish and season with salt and pepper. Bring to the boil, then cover tightly with a piece of damp greaseproof paper and the lid. Simmer gently for 10 minutes or until cooked. Meanwhile, steam the vegetables or sauté in oil until tender. Serve topped with the fish and juices.

Watchpoints

• In order to fillet fish at home, you must have a proper sharp filleting knife with a long flexible blade which will glide over the bones as you cut. If your knife is blunt or too short you will inevitably leave a lot of flesh attached to the bones.

• You will get four fillets from a flat fish, which should be skinned before filleting.
• Cook fillets as soon as they have been prepared, or wrap in cling film and store in the refrigerator until required, or they will dry out.

Cook's tip

To remove double fillets, that is just one fillet from each side of the fish, cut through to the bone in a semi-circle around the back of the head. Slide the knife in under the fish between flesh and bones, and work along one side, releasing the flesh from the bones in as far as the backbone. Turn the fish around and repeat on the other side. Detach the whole fillet, then turn the fish over and repeat on the other side.

Golden Crumbed Plaice

SERVES 4

255 CALORIES/SERVING

450 g (1 lb) plaice fillets (see page 76)
dash of lemon juice
1 bay leaf
salt and pepper
40 g (1½ oz) butter or margarine
50 g (2 oz) fresh brown breadcrumbs
3 celery sticks, roughly chopped
25 g (1 oz) chopped walnuts
30 ml (2 level tbsp) chopped fresh parsley
parsley sprigs, to garnish

1 If necessary, divide each fish fillet lengthways in half, then roll up with the skinned side inside. Secure with a cocktail stick.

2 Place the fish in a sauté pan, and add water to barely cover. Add the lemon juice and bay leaf, and season with salt and pepper. Bring slowly to the boil, cover and simmer very gently for about 5 minutes or until tender.

3 Meanwhile, melt the butter in a frying pan. Add the breadcrumbs and fry, stirring occasionally, until beginning to brown. Mix in the celery and walnuts, and cook until the crumbs are golden. Stir in the parsley and season with salt and pepper.

4 Drain the fish on absorbent kitchen paper. Remove the cocktail sticks. Serve immediately, topped with the golden crumbs and garnished with parsley.

Thai Grilled Caramelized Fish

SERVES 4

373 CALORIES/SERVING

8 plaice fillets (see page 76)

5 ml (1 level tsp) salt

juice of 2 limes

60–90 ml (4–6 level tbsp) demerara sugar

salad leaves, lime wedges and 5 ml (1 level tsp) finely chopped red chilli, to garnish

For the sweet and sour sauce

400 g (14 oz) red peppers, deseeded and chopped

50 g (2 oz) red chillies, deseeded and chopped

2 garlic cloves, chopped

30 ml (2 tbsp) olive oil

60 ml (4 level tbsp) sugar

90 ml (6 tbsp) distilled malt vinegar

1 To make the sauce, put the peppers, chillies and garlic in a blender or food processor with 30 ml (2 tbsp) water, and blend until smooth.

2 Put the remaining sauce ingredients in a saucepan. Add the red pepper and chilli paste, and 100 ml (4 fl oz) water. Bring to the boil, then lower the heat and simmer for about 20 minutes or until reduced by half.

3 Meanwhile, sprinkle each plaice fillet with salt and lime juice, and roll up. Secure with wooden cocktail sticks. Set aside for 30 minutes. Just before grilling, rub the fish all over with the sugar.

4 Cook the rolled fillets under the grill for 4–5 minutes on each side, or until cooked and caramelized. Remove the cocktail sticks.

5 Serve immediately on a bed of salad leaves and garnished with lime wedges and chopped red chilli. Accompany with the sweet and sour sauce.

Grilled Plaice with Mushrooms

SERVES 4

215 CALORIES/SERVING

25 g (1 oz) butter or margarine

225 g (8 oz) button mushrooms, wiped and finely chopped

125 g (4 oz) eating apple, peeled, cored and chopped

25 g (1 oz) fresh brown breadcrumbs

5 ml (1 level tsp) wholegrain mustard

30 ml (2 level tbsp) chopped fresh parsley

salt and pepper

4 double plaice fillets, about 125 g (4 oz) each (see page 76)

60 ml (4 tbsp) dry cider

apple slices, to garnish

1 Melt the butter in a small saucepan and sauté the mushrooms and apple for 2–3 minutes. Increase the heat and cook, stirring, for 1–2 minutes or until most of the excess liquid has evaporated. Remove from the heat.

2 Stir the breadcrumbs into the mushroom mixture with half the wholegrain mustard and the chopped parsley. Season with salt and pepper.

3 Lay the plaice fillets, skinned side up, on a flat surface and divide the mushroom mixture between them. Roll up the fillets with the stuffing inside, and secure with wooden cocktail sticks. Place the rolled plaice fillets, seam side down, in a small shallow flameproof dish.

4 Whisk together the remaining mustard and the cider, and spoon over the fish. Grill for about 10 minutes, turning occasionally and brushing with the mustard mixture.

5 Remove the cocktail sticks. Serve the fish immediately, garnished with apple slices.

Scallops

Fresh scallops are sold in their delicately coloured, fan-shaped shells. They are amongst the most expensive of shellfish, but their rich creaminess means a small amount goes a long way. The beautiful dark pink coral is considered a great delicacy.

Scallops au Gratin

SERVES 4

515 CALORIES/SERVING

8 large scallops
300 ml (½ pint) Cheese (Mornay) Sauce (see page 14)
60 ml (4 tbsp) dry white wine
salt and pepper
125 g (4 oz) mushrooms, wiped and sliced
175 g (6 oz) fresh white breadcrumbs
125 g (4 oz) butter, melted
juice of ½ lemon
lemon slices, to garnish

Watchpoints

• Scallops are best bought live in the shell. However, they are kept tightly closed by a strong muscle which makes them extremely difficult to prise open. It's advisable to get your fishmonger to open them. Don't forget to ask for the shells for serving.

• Large scallops are usually sliced for cooking, while smaller ones are left whole. Like prawns, they need only brief cooking or they will be tough. The delicate orange coral takes a matter of seconds to cook so this is usually separated and added last.

1 Scrub the scallop shells under cold running water to remove as much sand as possible. Give any that are open a sharp tap with the back of a knife. Discard any that do not close. Put a scallop flat side up on a board or hold it level in the palm of your hand. Insert the point of a strong knife (with a blade about 10 cm/4 inches long) between the shells at about 45° to the hinge. (It probably won't go straight in but be patient and continue pushing and twisting until it does.)

2 When the shells have opened slightly, slide your finger in between the shells (it's a good idea to wear a sturdy glove for this), then with the knife in your other hand quickly cut round the top shell to detach the muscle and allow the shells to be parted. Push the top shell backwards until the hinge at the back snaps. Rinse the scallop (still attached to the lower shell) under cold running water to remove any sand.

3 Using a small knife and being careful not to tear the flesh, cut away all the grey coloured beard-like fringe.

4 Slide the point of a knife under the black thread on the side of the scallop. Gently pull it off with the attached intestinal bag. Ease the scallop away from the bottom shell and take out the white meat and coral. Scrub the rounded shells and sterilize in boiling water, then dry.

5 Coat the inside of each rounded shell with some of the Mornay Sauce. Sprinkle with wine. Lay a scallop in each shell and season with salt and pepper.

6 Surround the scallops with mushrooms and cover with the remaining sauce. Sprinkle with the breadcrumbs and butter. Place the shells on a baking sheet and bake in the oven at 200°C (400°F) mark 6 for about 10 minutes. Sprinkle with a little lemon juice, garnish with lemon slices and serve.

Scallops in Creamy Basil Sauce

SERVES 4

535 CALORIES/SERVING

900 g (2 lb) shelled scallops (see page 81)
30 ml (2 tbsp) oil
15 g (½ oz) butter
1 small onion, peeled and finely chopped
2 garlic cloves, crushed
150 ml (¼ pint) dry white wine
20 ml (4 level tsp) chopped fresh basil
salt and pepper
150 ml (5 fl oz) carton double cream
basil sprigs, to garnish

1 Cut the scallops, including the coral, into fairly thick slices.

2 Heat the oil and butter in a large frying pan, add the onion and garlic, and fry gently for 5 minutes or until soft and lightly coloured.

3 Add the scallops to the pan and toss to coat in the oil and butter. Stir in the wine and basil, and season with salt and pepper. Cook over a moderate heat for 2–3 minutes or until the scallops are tender, turning them

constantly so that they cook evenly on all sides. Do not overcook or they will become tough and rubbery.

4 Remove the scallops from the liquid with a slotted spoon and set aside on a plate. Boil the liquid until reduced by about half, then stir in the cream, a little at a time, and simmer until the sauce is thick.

5 Return the scallops to the pan and heat gently. Taste and adjust the seasoning and serve garnished with basil.

Glazed Seafood Platter

SERVES 6

440 CALORIES/SERVING

225 g (8 oz) haddock fillet, skinned
450 g (1 lb) halibut fillet, skinned
75 g (3 oz) fennel
300 ml (½ pint) dry white wine
150 ml (¼ pint) fish stock
1 bay leaf
225 g (8 oz) queen scallops, shelled (see page 81)
125 g (4 oz) cooked shelled mussels (see page 75)
125 g (4 oz) cooked peeled prawns
40 g (1½ oz) butter
40 g (1½ oz) white plain flour
1 egg yolk
150 ml (5 fl oz) carton double cream
salt and pepper
50 g (2 oz) Emmenthal cheese, coarsely grated

1 Cut the haddock and halibut fillets into bite-sized pieces. Remove the feathery tops from the fennel, finely chop and reserve. Cut the fennel into wafer-thin slices.

2 Place the fish and fennel in a sauté pan or frying pan and pour on the wine and stock. Add the bay leaf. Bring to the boil, then reduce the heat, cover and simmer for 7–8 minutes or until the fish is just cooked.

3 With a slotted spoon, remove the fish and fennel from the cooking liquor and arrange in a single layer in a large gratin dish.

4 Add the scallops and mussels to the liquid, return to the boil and immediately remove with a slotted spoon. Scatter over the fish with the prawns. Cover the platter with foil and keep warm in the oven at 170°C (325°F) mark 3.

5 Melt the butter in a saucepan. Stir in the flour and cook, stirring, for 1–2 minutes. Remove from the heat and gradually strain in the cooking liquor, stirring constantly. Bring to the boil, stirring all the time, then reduce the heat and simmer for 2–3 minutes or until thickened. Beat in the egg yolk, cream, and salt and pepper to taste.

6 Spoon the sauce evenly over the seafood and sprinkle with the cheese. Place the platter under a hot grill until golden brown. Serve immediately, garnished with the reserved fennel tops.

Cook's tip

There are several types of scallop, which vary in size. The common great scallop can be as large as 15 cm (6 inches) across, while smaller queen scallops, or 'queenies', are usually about 7.5 cm (3 inches) across.

Scallops with Ginger

SERVES 3

280 CALORIES/SERVING

450 g (1 lb) shelled large scallops (see page 81)
4 celery sticks
bunch of spring onions
25 g (1 oz) piece of fresh root ginger
2 large garlic cloves
30 ml (2 tbsp) oil
1.25 ml (¼ level tsp) chilli powder
30 ml (2 tbsp) lemon juice
30 ml (2 tbsp) soy sauce
45 ml (3 level tbsp) chopped fresh coriander
salt and pepper

1 Cut the scallops, including the coral, into 5 mm (¼ inch) slices. Slice the celery and onions diagonally. Peel and slice the ginger and garlic.

2 Heat the oil in a large wok or frying pan. Add the scallops, vegetables, ginger, garlic and chilli powder, and stir-fry over a high heat for 2 minutes or until just tender.

3 Pour in the lemon juice and soy sauce, allow to bubble up, then stir in about 30 ml (2 tbsp) chopped coriander. Season with salt and pepper and serve immediately, topped with more coriander.

MEAT AND POULTRY

———◆———

Although some people now avoid meat in favour of other lower-fat protein foods, it is still a major component of most people's diet. When planning meals, especially for entertaining, it is still usual to base the meal around a main meat dish. The techniques and recipes featured in this chapter are those you might well choose for entertaining – an impressive crown roast of lamb; succulent steaks; tender pork fillet.

Chicken is a perennial favourite and often the first choice for entertaining. Moving on from everyday roasts and chicken breast recipes, this chapter shows you firstly how to bone a whole chicken, then how to stuff and cook it. The recipes that follow make use of these techniques and include an unusual Thai recipe in which the boned chicken is stuffed with duck breasts and minced pork flavoured with ginger, chillies and garlic.

Rack of Lamb

A cut of meat trimmed from the best end of neck of lamb, rack of lamb forms the basis of some of the most famous and spectacular roast meat dishes, namely crown roasts and guards of honour. Rack of lamb can also be roasted plain, with a simple herb and breadcrumb coating, to create a delicious Sunday lunch dish. All that's needed for preparing the rack is a small, sharp cook's knife, a chopping board and a little patience.

Roast Rack of Lamb

SERVES 6

280 CALORIES/SERVING

2 best end necks of lamb, about 1 kg (2¼ lb) each
salt and pepper
For the coating
finely grated rind of 1 lemon
125 g (4 oz) fresh white breadcrumbs
60 ml (4 level tbsp) chopped fresh parsley
15 ml (1 level tbsp) olive paste or finely chopped black olives
1 small egg, beaten
olive oil
gravy, to accompany

VARIATION

Garlic Lamb
Divide each prepared rack into three, make cuts in the fat and fill with slices of garlic. Place in a roasting tin and drizzle with olive oil. Season well and top with sprigs of rosemary. Roast at 200°C (400°F) mark 6 for about 25 minutes for medium rare, a little longer for well done.

1 Prepare one rack at a time. Place the lamb, fat side down, on a board. Using a small, sharp cook's knife, carefully remove the chine bone from the eye of the meat (the central round of meat). Keep the knife close to the bone so that as little meat as possible is removed with it.

2 Cut away the yellow strip of connective tissue at the base of the eye of the meat. With the point of the knife, slit open the side of the neck, between the skin and the eye, and ease out the shoulder blade (a small, flat, disc shape, not shown). Sometimes the butcher will remove this.

3 Turn the lamb over. Cut right through the skin and meat about 2.5 cm (1 inch) up from the tips of the bones, in a line parallel to the eye of the meat. This will leave about 9–10 cm (3½–4 inches) of flesh on the bones. Pull off the top strip of fatty meat to expose the bones.

4 Cut out the meat and fat between the bones and then scrape the bones completely clean. Trim all skin (sometimes the butcher will already have removed this) and most of the fat off the meat. Leave a thin covering of fat only. Using the tip of the knife, lightly score the fat into a diamond pattern. Grind black pepper over the fat and sprinkle with salt. Prepare the second rack of lamb in the same way.

5 Preheat the oven to 200°C (400°F) mark 6. To prepare the crumb coating for the lamb, mix the lemon rind with the breadcrumbs, parsley, olive paste, egg and 15 ml (1 tbsp) oil. Season with salt and pepper, then carefully press the crumb mixture on to the fatty side of the lamb. Place the racks in a large roasting tin with the crumb side uppermost. Drizzle 45 ml (3 tbsp) oil over the crumbs.

6 Place the tin in the centre of the oven. Cook for 35–40 minutes for rare; 40–45 minutes for medium rare; 45–50 minutes for well done. Baste once during cooking, then cover loosely with foil to stop the crust from burning. To test the meat, pierce the eye with a skewer. If the juices run red, it will be rare and if they run clear, it will be well done. To serve, slice the racks into three and accompany with gravy.

Crown Roast of Lamb (page 88)

Watchpoints

• Tie crown roasts and guards of honour firmly with string or they might burst open when cooking.
• Thoroughly scrape clean the bones before roasting or they might become charred. Cover exposed bones with foil before cooking.

Freezer notes

To freeze: Using fresh lamb only, freeze after step 4.
To use: Thaw, loosely wrapped, at cool room temperature overnight.

Buying guide

Each best end of neck will have seven or sometimes eight cutlet bones and should weigh about 1 kg (2 ¼ lb) before trimming. Buy them with long cutlet bones; the whole joint should be about 13.5–15 cm (5 ½–6 inches) long. It's important to ask the butcher to saw through the chine bone (backbone) just where it meets the cutlet bones, taking care not to cut into the eye of the meat. It's hazardous to do at home unless you have a small sharp meat saw.

Crown Roast of Lamb

SERVES 6

700 CALORIES/SERVING

2 best end necks of lamb, about 1.4 kg (3 lb) total weight
40 g (1½ oz) butter or margarine
1 large onion, peeled and chopped
4 celery sticks, chopped
1 large eating apple, peeled, cored and chopped
50 g (2 oz) no-soak dried apricots, chopped
150 g (5 oz) fresh breadcrumbs
30 ml (2 level tbsp) chopped fresh parsley
finely grated rind of ½ large lemon
25 ml (5 tsp) lemon juice
1 egg, beaten
salt and pepper
15–30 ml (1–2 tbsp) olive oil
15 ml (1 level tbsp) white plain flour
300 ml (½ pint) lamb stock

1 Prepare the racks of lamb as in steps 1–4 of Roast Rack of Lamb (see page 86). Bend the joints around and tie them securely together, fat side inside.

2 Melt the butter in a saucepan and cook the onion, celery and apple until brown. Stir in the apricots, breadcrumbs, parsley, lemon rind and juice and egg, and season with salt and pepper. Allow to cool.

3 Fill the centre of the joint with the stuffing and weigh. Place in a small roasting tin and spoon over the oil. Cover exposed bones with foil. Roast in the oven at 200°C (400°F) mark 6 for 20 minutes per 450 g (1 lb) plus an extra 20 minutes, basting occasionally and covering with foil if necessary.

4 Remove the foil, transfer the crown roast to a warmed serving dish and keep it warm. Drain off as much fat as possible from the roasting tin, add the flour and blend well. Cook for 1 minute, stirring, then stir in the stock and cook for 2–3 minutes. Season to taste and serve hot with the joint.

Crown Roast with Provençal Vegetables

SERVES 6

360 CALORIES/SERVING

1 large aubergine
salt and pepper
olive oil
350 g (12 oz) onion, peeled and roughly chopped
1 red pepper, deseeded and sliced into matchstick pieces
1 yellow pepper, deseeded and sliced into matchstick pieces
450 g (1 lb) courgettes, cut into 5 mm (¼ inch) thick slices
400 g (14 oz) can chopped tomatoes
45 ml (3 level tbsp) chopped fresh mint
2 garlic cloves, crushed
400 g (14 oz) can artichoke hearts, drained and halved
2 best end necks of lamb, about 1 kg (2¼ lb) each
20 ml (4 level tsp) Dijon mustard
gravy, to accompany
mint leaves, to garnish

1 Slice the aubergine into 5 mm (¼ inch) thick pieces (quarter if large). Sprinkle with salt and leave to drain in a colander for about 30 minutes. Rinse off the salt and pat dry with absorbent kitchen paper.

2 Heat 45 ml (3 tbsp) oil in a large flameproof casserole. Add the aubergine and stir-fry for 3–4 minutes. Add the onion, peppers and courgettes, and stir-fry for a further 3–4 minutes. Mix in the tomatoes, mint and garlic, and season with salt and pepper. Cover and simmer for 10–15 minutes or until the vegetables are beginning to soften. Stir in the artichokes and set aside.

3 Prepare the racks of lamb as in steps 1–4 of Roast Rack of Lamb (see page 86). Bend the joints around and tie them securely together, fat side inside. Weigh the joint. Fill the centre of the crown with foil to push the joints into a neat crown shape, and cover all the cutlet bones with foil to prevent them from burning. Spread the mustard evenly all over the exposed meat flesh.

4 Place the crown in a roasting tin with a little oil. Roast in the oven at 200°C (400°F) mark 6 for 20 minutes per 450 g (1 lb), plus an extra 20 minutes for medium-rare lamb; a little longer if you prefer it well done. After 40 minutes, remove the centre foil and fill the crown with

the provençal vegetables. Drizzle with oil and return to the oven to finish cooking. Reheat the rest of the vegetables separately, simmering gently until tender.

5 Remove the foil from the bones and lift the crown on to a serving dish. Serve with the remaining vegetables and gravy made from the pan juices. Garnish with the fresh mint leaves.

Golden-Crusted Guard of Honour

SERVES 6

490 CALORIES/SERVING

2 best end necks of lamb, about 1 kg (2¼ lb) each
900 g (2 lb) medium-sized old potatoes
90 ml (6 tbsp) olive oil
450 g (1 lb) onions, peeled and sliced
10 ml (2 level tsp) dried thyme
salt and pepper
45 ml (3 level tbsp) tahini (sesame paste)
45 ml (3 level tbsp) sesame seeds
lemon juice
watercress sprigs and bay leaves, to garnish (optional)
gravy, to accompany

1 Prepare the racks of lamb as in steps 1–4 of Roast Rack of Lamb (see page 86). Stand the racks upright and interlace the bones, fat side outside. Tie three pieces of string right around the racks to hold them together. Weigh the joint, then cover the cutlet bones with foil.

2 Scrub the potatoes and slice them into 5 mm (¼ inch) thick pieces. Heat the oil in a large roasting tin. When it is hot, add the potatoes, onions and thyme. Season with salt and pepper, and mix well. Cook for 2–3 minutes.

3 Place a wire rack over the vegetables in the roasting tin and stand the lamb on top. Spread the tahini over the lamb fat and carefully sprinkle over the sesame seeds.

4 Roast the lamb in the oven at 200°C (400°F) mark 6 for 20 minutes per 450 g (1 lb) plus an extra 20 minutes for medium-rare lamb, a little longer if you like it well done. Stir the vegetables once during the cooking time. Just before serving, squeeze a little lemon juice over the lamb.

5 Serve the lamb surrounded by the onions and potatoes, and garnished with watercress sprigs and bay leaves, if wished. Accompany with a rich gravy made from the pan juices.

Steaks

Sliced from the tenderest cuts of beef, for those who love meat, a good steak is hard to beat. Steaks need very little preparation and are quick to cook, though they need careful watching to ensure they do not overcook.

Marinated Steaks with Red Wine

SERVES 2

430 CALORIES/SERVING

| two 175 g (6 oz) sirloin or fillet steaks, 1 cm (½ inch) thick |
| 2 small shallots |
| 2 garlic cloves |
| 150 ml (¼ pint) red wine |
| olive oil |
| salt and pepper |
| 2 bay leaves |
| 10 ml (2 level tsp) redcurrant jelly |
| 25 g (1 oz) butter |

1 Using a sharp cook's knife, carefully trim excess fat off the outside of each steak, leaving a thin covering so that the fat will melt into the steak and help to tenderize it. With the tip of the knife, very lightly score both sides of each steak. The marinade will be able to seep into the steaks through these cuts.

2 Prepare the marinade. Peel the shallots, then halve and finely chop them. Peel the garlic cloves, then cut them across into very fine slices. Whisk together the red wine, 15 ml (1 tbsp) olive oil and plenty of salt and pepper. Stir in the shallots, garlic and bay leaves. Select a glass or china dish, not metal, into which the steaks will just fit.

3 Place the steaks in the dish and pour the marinade over. Turn the steaks over and baste well with the marinade. Cover and refrigerate for at least 12 hours, turning just once. The longer you leave them, the stronger the flavour. Using draining spoons, lift the steaks out of the marinade and place on a plate; reserve the marinade.

Cook's tip
To test how well the steak is done, press gently with a spoon or clean finger. If rare, the steak will seem very soft and give readily to the pressure. If medium, it will seem firm on the outside but with plenty of 'give' in the centre. If well done, it will be completely firm with no give at all.

4 Brush a little oil over a small heavy-based frying pan, preferably ridged as this gives an attractive finish to the steak. Heat the frying pan and, when it is very hot, add the steaks and cook over a high heat, turning just once. Allow about 1 minute per side for rare steak, 2 minutes per side for medium-rare, 3 minutes per side for medium and 4 minutes per side for well done. Place on a heated plate and keep warm.

5 Allow the pan to cool slightly for about 1 minute. Add the redcurrant jelly and 60 ml (4 tbsp) water to the marinade. Pour into the pan and bring to the boil, stirring. Add the butter in small pieces, and bubble down until reduced by half, stirring occasionally. Season with salt and pepper.

6 Serve the steaks with seasonal vegetables and a little of the sauce spooned over each steak. Serve the remaining sauce separately.

Watchpoints

• To prevent steaks sticking to the pan, it's important to 'season' a new pan first. Heat with a little salt and about 5 mm (¼ inch) oil. Cool and leave for about 30 minutes. Always wipe out the pan after use with absorbent kitchen paper, never wash or scrub it.

• Lightly score the surface of steaks with a sharp cook's knife – not too deep.

• Never use a metallic dish for marinating as acids from the shallots and wine may react with the metal and affect the taste of the food.

• Always cover the steaks in the refrigerator or the strong marinating smells may taint other ingredients.

• Preheat the pan before frying the steaks; a cool pan will cause the steaks to stew rather than fry.

• To flavour steaks that haven't been marinated, season well with salt and pepper, then fry in a little olive oil with slices of garlic added to the pan.

Buying guide

Choosing a tender steak by sight is very difficult. Theoretically, if the meat is a deep claret colour and marbled with fat it should be tender, but this is not always the case. We tested dozens of sirloin steaks and found that top-quality butcher's sirloin steak was much more reliable than that from supermarkets, but this was reflected in the price. So if you're cooking for a special occasion and shop at a supermarket, it's probably best to opt for fillet steak, if possible.

Marinating steaks for a day or two (see recipe) does help to tenderize them, but won't cure a very tough one. Buy steaks with a thin covering of fat and about 1 cm (½ inch) thick; very thin steaks can become hard on cooking.

Steak au Poivre with Madeira (page 92)

Steak au Poivre with Madeira

Crush peppercorns finely – the coarser they are, the hotter they seem.

SERVES 2

420 CALORIES/SERVING

two 175 g (6 oz) sirloin or fillet steaks, 1 cm (½ inch) thick

7.5 ml (1½ level tsp) mixed dried peppercorns (green, red and black)

2 small shallots, peeled and finely chopped

hazelnut oil

60 ml (4 tbsp) Madeira

salt

25 g (1 oz) butter

asparagus, to garnish

potato straws, to accompany

1 Prepare the steaks as in step 1 of Marinated Steaks with Red Wine (see page 90).

2 Crush the peppercorns with a pestle and mortar or the end of a rolling pin, and press them on to each side of the steaks. Place the steaks in a non-metallic marinating dish.

3 Mix the shallots with 15 ml (1 tbsp) hazelnut oil and the Madeira, and add a little salt. Pour over the steaks, cover and refrigerate for at least 12 hours, turning the steaks once.

4 Lift the steaks out of the marinade and cook as in step 4 of Marinated Steaks with Red Wine. Reserve the marinade.

5 Allow the pan to cool slightly for about 1 minute. Add 90 ml (6 tbsp) water to the marinade. Pour into the pan, then stir in the butter in small pieces. Bring to the boil, stirring occasionally, and bubble down until slightly reduced. Adjust the seasoning. Spoon a little sauce over the steaks and serve the remainder separately. Garnish with asparagus and accompany with potato straws.

Pan-fried Steaks with Herby Potatoes

SERVES 4

320 CALORIES/SERVING

700 g (1½ lb) small new potatoes, halved

125 g (4 oz) shallots or onions, peeled and finely chopped

salt

30 ml (2 tbsp) olive oil

1 garlic clove, crushed

125 g (4 oz) dolcelatte or cambazola cheese, diced

15 ml (1 level tbsp) chopped fresh thyme

four 175 g (6 oz) sirloin or fillet steaks

watercress, to garnish

1 Cook the potatoes and shallots together in boiling salted water for 4–5 minutes or until the potatoes are almost tender. Drain well.

2 Toss the potatoes and shallots in the olive oil with the garlic. Place in a flat, heatproof dish or on a baking sheet. Cook under a hot grill for 5–7 minutes or until crisp and brown. Dot with the cheese and return to the grill for 1–2 minutes or until melted and golden. Sprinkle with chopped thyme.

3 Pan-fry the steaks as described in step 4 of Marinated Steaks with Red Wine (see page 90). Serve immediately, garnished with watercress and accompanied by the potatoes.

Cook's tip

Before pan-frying the steaks, tie a rasher of rindless, smoked streaky bacon around each one to give them a delicious smoky flavour.

Mustard Steaks with Mushrooms and Cream

SERVES 2

450 CALORIES/SERVING

two 175 g (6 oz) sirloin or fillet steaks, 1 cm (½ inch) thick

20 ml (4 level tsp) Dijon mustard

2 garlic cloves, crushed

salt and pepper

2 small shallots, peeled and finely chopped

olive oil

60 ml (4 tbsp) brandy

90 ml (6 tbsp) single cream

75 g (3 oz) mixed mushrooms, preferably wild

French bread croûtes, to serve (optional)

fresh tarragon, to garnish

1 Prepare the steaks as in step 1 of Marinated Steaks with Red Wine (see page 90).

2 Mix together the mustard and garlic, season with salt and pepper, and spread over the steaks. Place the steaks in a non-metallic marinating dish.

3 Mix the shallots with 15 ml (1 tbsp) olive oil and the brandy. Pour over the steaks, cover and refrigerate for at least 12 hours, turning the steaks once.

4 Lift the steaks out of the marinade and cook as in step 4 of Marinated Steaks with Red Wine. Reserve the marinade.

5 Allow the pan to cool slightly for about 1 minute. Add the cream and 60 ml (4 tbsp) water to the marinade, and pour into the pan. Add the mushrooms and bring to the boil, stirring occasionally. Bubble down until slightly reduced. Taste and adjust the seasoning.

6 Serve the steaks on croûtes of French bread, if wished. Spoon a little sauce over each steak and serve the remainder separately. Garnish with fresh tarragon.

Pork Fillet

Also known as pork tenderloin, fillet of pork is a lean and tender cut that is ideal for slicing and stir-frying, though it can also be stuffed and roasted whole.

Normandy Pork

SERVES 6

472 CALORIES/SERVING

900 g (2 lb) pork fillet
300 ml (½ pint) dry white wine
225 g (8 oz) button mushrooms, wiped and sliced
30 ml (2 level tbsp) seasoned flour
25 g (1 oz) butter or margarine
15 ml (1 tbsp) vegetable oil
30 ml (2 tbsp) Calvados
2 large cooking apples, peeled, cored and thinly sliced
30 ml (2 level tbsp) chopped fresh parsley
150 ml (5 fl oz) carton double cream
salt and pepper

1 Trim the pork fillet of all visible fat and cut across into thick strips. Bring the wine to the boil in a small saucepan, add the mushrooms, and simmer, covered, for 10–15 minutes.

2 Put the seasoned flour in a dish, add the pork strips and toss until evenly coated. Heat the butter and oil in a large frying pan or flameproof dish, add the pork, and fry until browned.

3 Put the Calvados in a ladle and warm it gently.

4 Set the Calvados alight and, when the flames die down, pour it carefully over the meat.

5 Add the wine, mushrooms and apples to the pork and simmer, covered, for 30 minutes or until tender. Add the parsley and cream and simmer without boiling until the sauce thickens slightly. Season with salt and pepper, and serve.

Watchpoints
• Pork fillets rarely weigh much more than 450 g (1 lb) but as they are so lean there is very little wastage.
• When stir-frying, stir constantly while cooking to ensure even cooking.

Pork and Pasta Sauté

SERVES 4

445 CALORIES/SERVING

450 g (1 lb) pork fillet

4 streaky bacon rashers, derinded and chopped

2 red onions, peeled and finely sliced

15 ml (1 level tbsp) wholegrain mustard

100 ml (4 fl oz) dry cider

1 garlic clove, crushed

45–60 ml (3–4 tbsp) oil

salt and pepper

1 green pepper

175 g (6 oz) green beans, halved

75 g (3 oz) dried pasta shells or bows

15 ml (1 tbsp) soy sauce

60 ml (4 tbsp) light stock

1 Trim the pork and cut into strips measuring about 5 cm × 5 mm (2 × ¼ inch), discarding any excess fat.

2 Put the pork, bacon and onions in a bowl. Add the mustard, cider, garlic and 15 ml (1 tbsp) oil. Season with salt and pepper and stir well. Cover and leave to marinate in the refrigerator for at least 1 hour, preferably overnight.

3 Halve, core and deseed the green pepper, then cut into strips. Blanch the green beans and pepper together in boiling salted water for 2 minutes. Drain, rinse under cold running water and leave to cool completely.

4 Cook the pasta in boiling salted water for 7–10 minutes or until just tender. Drain and toss in a little oil to prevent the pasta sticking.

5 Remove the pork, bacon and onions from the marinade, reserving the marinade. Heat 30 ml (2 tbsp) oil in a large sauté pan or frying pan, add the meat and sauté over a high heat for 3–4 minutes or until lightly browned.

6 Stir in the beans and green pepper with the marinade, soy sauce and stock. Season with pepper. Bring to the boil, stirring, then simmer gently for about 4 minutes. Add the pasta and cook for 1 minute or until piping hot. Serve immediately.

Sautéed Pork in Citrus Sauce

SERVES 2

585 CALORIES/SERVING

225 g (8 oz) pork fillet

seasoned flour for coating

juice of 1 small orange

juice of 1 small grapefruit

60 ml (4 tbsp) dry white wine

15 ml (1 level tbsp) chopped fresh coriander

15 ml (1 tbsp) oil

25 g (1 oz) butter

pinch of paprika

90 ml (6 tbsp) double cream

salt and pepper

orange and grapefruit slices and fresh coriander, to garnish

1 Trim the pork of all visible fat and cut into 5 mm (¼ inch) thick slices. Place between two sheets of greaseproof paper or cling film, and beat out into thin slices with a meat mallet or rolling pin. Dip the pork slices in the seasoned flour to coat.

2 Put 30 ml (2 tbsp) orange juice and 30 ml (2 tbsp) grapefruit juice in a small saucepan. Add the wine and chopped coriander, bring to the boil, and boil until reduced by half.

3 Meanwhile, heat the oil and butter in a sauté pan and fry the pork slices for 2 minutes on each side or until cooked through.

4 Add the juice mixture, paprika and cream to the pan, and simmer gently for 1–2 minutes or until heated through. Season with salt and pepper. Garnish with citrus slices and coriander, and serve at once.

Stir-fried Pork with Baby Corn

SERVES 4

300 CALORIES/SERVING

450 g (1 lb) pork fillet

175 g (6 oz) carrots, peeled

175 g (6 oz) baby corn cobs

175 g (6 oz) sugar-snap peas

salt and pepper

45 ml (3 tbsp) sunflower oil

60 ml (4 tbsp) stir-fry chilli and tomato sauce (see Cook's tip)

5 ml (1 level tsp) caster sugar

30 ml (2 tbsp) wine vinegar

60 ml (4 tbsp) light soy sauce

chives and parsley sprigs, to garnish

1 Trim the pork of all visible fat and cut into 5 mm (¼ inch) thick slices. Cut the carrots into sticks. Blanch the vegetables in boiling salted water for 2 minutes, then drain and refresh under cold running water. Drain again thoroughly.
2 Heat the oil in a large wok or frying pan (preferably non-stick). Add the pork and stir-fry over a high heat for 2–3 minutes or until well browned and almost tender.

3 Add the vegetables to the pan and continue stirring over a high heat for 2–3 minutes or until piping hot.
4 Mix in the remaining ingredients and bring to the boil, stirring well. Adjust the seasoning and serve, garnished with chives and parsley.

Cook's tip

Bottled chilli and tomato sauce is available from delicatessens and larger supermarkets.

Pork Chasseur

SERVES 4

440 CALORIES/SERVING

700 g (1½ lb) pork fillet

30 ml (2 tbsp) olive oil

25 g (1 oz) butter

2 shallots or 1 small onion, peeled and finely chopped

175 g (6 oz) button mushrooms, wiped

15 ml (1 tbsp) white plain flour

100 ml (4 fl oz) dry white wine

30 ml (2 tbsp) brandy

15 ml (1 level tbsp) tomato purée

300 ml (½ pint) chicken or veal stock

30 ml (2 level tbsp) chopped fresh sage

salt and pepper

sage sprigs, to garnish

1 Trim the pork fillet of all visible fat and cut into 1 cm (½ inch) thick slices.
2 Heat the oil in a large frying pan, add the pork slices and fry over a high heat for about 5 minutes or until browned on both sides. Remove the pork from the pan with a slotted spoon and set aside.
3 Add the butter to the pan and fry the shallots for 3 minutes. Add the mushrooms and cook for 2–3 minutes, then stir in the flour. Cook for 1 minute, stirring, then remove from the heat and gradually stir in the white wine, brandy, tomato purée and stock. Bring to the boil, stirring constantly.
4 Return the pork to the pan with the sage. Season with salt and pepper, cover and simmer for 15–20 minutes or until the pork is cooked. Transfer to a warmed serving dish and serve garnished with sage sprigs.

Boned Chicken

Boned chicken can be time-consuming to prepare but with practice you'll speed up. The end result is wonderfully tasty and looks stunning when elegantly sliced.

Party Chicken

SERVES 8 (AS PART OF A BUFFET)

425 CALORIES/SERVING

15 ml (1 tbsp) olive oil
2 shallots, peeled and finely chopped
450 g (1 lb) good-quality pork sausages
75 g (3 oz) toasted nuts, roughly chopped
finely grated rind of 1 lemon
60 ml (4 level tbsp) chopped fresh parsley
20 ml (4 level tsp) Dijon mustard
salt and pepper
50 g (2 oz) lean sliced cooked ham
50 g (2 oz) sliced tongue
1.8 kg (4 lb) oven-ready chicken
50 g (2 oz) pitted black olives, halved
50 g (2 oz) butter
300 ml (½ pint) chicken stock
tomato chutney, to accompany

Cook's tip
If you haven't much time, ask your butcher to bone a chicken for you. Boned chicken is an economical choice for entertaining as stuffing and rolling makes it go a lot further.

1 First prepare the stuffing. Heat the oil in a small frying pan, add the shallots, and fry until golden. Leave to cool. Skin the sausages and mix with the shallots, nuts, lemon rind, parsley, mustard and plenty of seasoning. Cut the ham and tongue into strips.

2 Place the chicken, breast side down, on a board. Cut along the backbone. Keeping the blade close to the bones to avoid piercing the flesh, scrape the flesh and skin away from one side of the rib cage. Cut out the exposed bone above the wing joint. Separate the leg and wing ball-and-socket joints and push apart.

3 Repeat the process on the other side of the rib cage. Lift the exposed rib cage in one hand and carefully fillet the flesh away from the breastbone. Reserve the rib bones for stock (see Watchpoints). Next, cut through the flesh, down the length of the leg and ease the bones out, discarding the knuckles.

4 Cut off the end two joints of each wing. Cut through the skin to expose the remaining wing joint and ease out the bone. You should now have a large rectangle of skin covered in chicken flesh. Place the boned chicken, skin side down, on the board. Cover with cling film and bat lightly with a rolling pin to give an even covering of flesh.

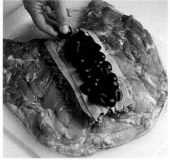

5 Spoon half the stuffing down the centre of the bird. Arrange the ham, tongue and olives on top and carefully top with the remaining stuffing. Fold the skin over the stuffing and sew up the bird with cotton to give a neat sausage shape. Spread the chicken with butter and season well with salt and pepper.

6 Roll the chicken in a piece of muslin and tie the ends like a cracker. Place on a wire rack over a roasting tin. Pour the stock into the tin and bake in the oven at 190°C (375°F) mark 5 for about 1¾ hours, basting occasionally. When cooked, remove the muslin and place the chicken on a plate. Cool, cover and refrigerate for several hours to firm up. Ease out any cotton used to sew up the chicken skin. Slice thickly and serve with salad leaves and tomato chutney.

Watchpoints

• Use a very sharp, small cook's knife as a blunt blade can damage the skin.
• Work carefully when boning, especially when you reach the breastbone, as it's important not to puncture the skin. The stuffing will ooze out through any holes.

• If the skin is damaged, sew up any holes before stuffing. Use brightly coloured cotton as it's easier to see to remove later.
• Reserve all chicken bones as these can be used to make stock. Cover with water and simmer with vegetables and seasoning for about 1 hour.

• Run your fingers over the boned flesh to ensure no stray bones remain.
• Cooking the chicken in muslin keeps it moist. Or use a blue J-cloth – not pink as the colour may run.
• Test the chicken with a fine skewer. The juices will run clear when it is cooked.

Freezer notes

To freeze: Overwrap and freeze the whole cooked chicken after chilling.
To use: Thaw overnight at cool room temperature. Chill before slicing.

Summer Chicken

SERVES 6

540 CALORIES/SERVING

butter
225 g (8 oz) brown-cap mushrooms, wiped and finely chopped
2 shallots, peeled and finely chopped
350 g (12 oz) trimmed leeks, roughly chopped
1 garlic clove, crushed
25 g (1 oz) medium oatmeal
finely grated rind and juice of 1 lemon
90 ml (6 level tbsp) chopped fresh parsley
30 ml (2 level tbsp) chopped fresh tarragon or 2.5 ml (½ level tsp) dried tarragon
50 g (2 oz) fresh breadcrumbs
salt and pepper
225 g (8 oz) rindless smoked streaky bacon
225 g (8 oz) young leaf spinach
1.8 kg (4 lb) oven-ready chicken
50 g (2 oz) sundried tomatoes in oil, drained and sliced
150 ml (¼ pint) white wine
300 ml (½ pint) stock
fresh herbs, to garnish

1 Heat 75 g (3 oz) butter in a large sauté pan, add the mushrooms, shallots, leeks and garlic, and fry until the excess moisture has evaporated. Leave to cool.

2 Grill the oatmeal until golden, and mix with the mushroom mixture, lemon rind, 15 ml (1 tbsp) lemon juice, herbs and breadcrumbs. Season with salt and pepper.

3 Grill the bacon and leave to cool. Cook the spinach leaves, a quarter at a time, in boiling salted water for about 10 seconds. Lift out with draining spoons and place in a colander. Immediately run cold water over the leaves. Drain and pat them gently with absorbent kitchen paper.

4 Bone and bat out the chicken as in steps 2, 3 and 4 of Party Chicken (see page 98). Spread with one-third of the stuffing, and top with a layer of spinach, bacon and sundried tomatoes. Spread with another third of the stuffing, the remaining spinach, etc., and finally cover with the remaining stuffing.

5 Sew up as in step 5 of Party Chicken, spread with 50 g (2 oz) butter, season well, then wrap and bake as in step 6 of Party Chicken, adding the wine and stock to the roasting tin.

6 When cooked, remove the muslin and place the chicken on a plate. Cool, cover and refrigerate for several hours to firm up. Slice thickly and serve garnished with fresh herbs.

Thai Spiced Chicken

SERVES 8

350 CALORIES/SERVING

oil
40 g (1½ oz) fresh root ginger, peeled and finely chopped
bunch of spring onions, roughly chopped
2 small green chillies, deseeded and finely chopped
1 large garlic clove, crushed
2.5 ml (½ level tsp) Thai seven-spice seasoning
350 g (12 oz) minced pork
50 g (2 oz) fresh breadcrumbs
salt and pepper
225 g (8 oz) duckling breast fillets, skinned
1 large red pepper
1.8 kg (4 lb) oven-ready chicken
1 shallot, peeled and finely chopped
90 ml (6 tbsp) Madeira
30 ml (2 tbsp) garlic vinegar
45 ml (3 tbsp) runny honey
50 g (2 oz) butter
300 ml (½ pint) chicken stock
fresh herbs, to garnish

1 First prepare the stuffing. Heat 30 ml (2 tbsp) oil in a frying pan, add the ginger, onions, chillies, garlic and seven-spice seasoning, and fry for 3–4 minutes, stirring occasionally. Allow to cool.

2 Mix the pork and breadcrumbs into the ginger mixture, and season with salt and pepper. Slice each duckling fillet into four thinnish pieces.

3 Grill the red pepper until blackened all over. Hold under cold running water and pull off the skin. Halve, deseed and slice.

4 Bone and bat out the chicken as in steps 2, 3 and 4 of Party Chicken (see page 98). Spread with half the stuffing. Lay the duckling breasts and pepper slices on top, and cover with the remaining stuffing. Sew up as in step 5 of Party Chicken.

5 Place the chicken in a non-metallic dish. Mix the shallot with the Madeira, vinegar, 30 ml (2 tbsp) oil and the honey. Season with salt and pepper, and spoon over the chicken. Cover and refrigerate for about 12 hours.

6 Lift the chicken out of the marinade. Spread with butter, then wrap and bake as in step 6 of Party Chicken, cooking for about 2 hours and occasionally basting with the marinade mixed with the stock. Cover loosely with foil, if necessary.

7 Remove the muslin and place the chicken on a plate. Bubble down the cooking juices to a glaze and brush over the chicken. Cool, cover and refrigerate for several hours to firm up.

8 Serve sliced, garnished with herbs.

Chicken Galantine

SERVES 6–8

530–400 CALORIES/SERVING

50 g (2 oz) butter or margarine
125 g (4 oz) button mushrooms, wiped and roughly chopped
1 onion, peeled and roughly chopped
3 celery sticks, roughly chopped
225 g (8 oz) fresh breadcrumbs
5 ml (1 level tsp) dried marjoram
1 egg, beaten
salt and pepper
1.4 kg (3 lb) oven-ready chicken, boned (see page 98)
125 g (4 oz) piece of garlic sausage

1 Melt half the butter in a large frying pan, add the vegetables and fry for about 4 minutes, then leave to cool.

2 Place the breadcrumbs in a bowl with the marjoram and cooked vegetables. Mix well with a wooden spoon, adding enough egg to bind. Season well with salt and pepper.

3 Spread the bird out, skin side down, on a board, and spoon some of the stuffing into the leg and wing cavities. Spread the remaining stuffing over the bird. Place the garlic sausage lengthways down the centre. Fold over the skin and sew up the bird as in step 5 of Party Chicken (see page 98).

4 Weigh the chicken and calculate the cooking time, allowing 25 minutes per 450 g (1 lb). Place the chicken in a roasting tin and dot with the remaining butter. Season well. Roast in the oven at 180°C (350°F) mark 4, basting frequently. When cooked, remove from the tin and leave to cool. Chill in the refrigerator. To serve, remove the thread and thinly slice the chicken.

DESSERTS

This chapter takes some of the most popular and enduring desserts and brings them right up to date. The choice ranges from luxurious crème brûlée and lemon syllabub to not-so-traditional steamed sponge puddings. In fact, the 'steamed' puddings featured are 'steam/baked', giving a lighter result more suited to today's tastes.

Cold, sweet soufflés are simple to make if you follow the instructions given in this chapter. They can be light and refreshing, like Lemon Soufflé, or rich and luscious, like the Double Chocolate Soufflé on page 114.

The chapter closes with a selection of Christmas puddings. A traditional rich Christmas pudding is followed by some more up to date and unusual alternatives – an Iced Christmas Pudding and a Rich Figgy Pudding. Whichever recipe you choose, its ideal accompaniment will be the Brandy Butter on page 123.

Crème Brûlée

Crème Brûlée, literally burnt cream, is said to have originated at Trinity College, Cambridge, over a century ago. Variations of this recipe must have appeared on every restaurant menu in Britain, ranging from the sublime to the very ordinary. Ours is of the sublime variety.

Crème Brûlée

SERVES 6

570 CALORIES/SERVING

1 vanilla pod (see Cook's tips on page 106) or 5 ml (1 tsp) vanilla essence
568 ml (1 pint) carton double cream
6 egg yolks
40 g (1½ oz) caster sugar
125 g (4 oz) granulated sugar
compote of soft summer fruit, to accompany (optional)

1 Split open the vanilla pod to reveal the seeds, then place in a medium saucepan with the cream. Bring slowly to just below the boil. Take off the heat, cover and leave to infuse for about 30 minutes. Lift out the pod. Scrape out the seeds and return them to the cream. Rinse and dry the pod; store in sugar as a flavouring.

2 Meanwhile, place the egg yolks in a medium bowl with the caster sugar and vanilla essence, if using. Beat the ingredients with a wooden spoon or an electric whisk until they've thickened and lightened in colour. Pour on the cream, stirring. Rinse the saucepan, then return the cream mixture to it.

3 Cook the custard over a gentle heat, stirring all the time, until it thickens slightly to the consistency of single cream and will just coat the back of the spoon. This can take 10 minutes. Watch the froth on the custard – as it begins to thicken, the froth disappears. Do not boil or the custard will curdle.

4 Strain the custard into a jug, gently rubbing the sieve with the back of the spoon to ensure all the vanilla seeds go through. Divide the custard among six 150 ml (¼ pint) ramekin dishes and place in a roasting tin. Pour hand-hot water into the roasting tin to come halfway up the sides of the ramekins.

5 Bake in the oven at 150°C (300°F) mark 2 for 30–35 minutes (see Cook's tips on page 106). The custard should have formed a skin on top and have firmed up slightly. To test, gently shake one ramekin; if the custard is set, it should have a slight wobble but not be at all runny. Bake for a little longer, if necessary. Cool, cover with cling film and chill for several hours.

6 Place half the granulated sugar in a small, heavy-based saucepan. Heat gently until the sugar dissolves and turns to a golden caramel. Immediately pour the caramel over three of the custards, tilting the dishes to give an even layer. Use the remaining sugar to make some more caramel and pour over the remaining three custards. Chill the brûlées, uncovered, for up to 6 hours.

Freezer notes

To freeze: Freeze at the end of step 5.

To use: Thaw at room temperature for about 4 hours. Chill and complete.

Watchpoints

• For maximum flavour, always scrape the seeds out of the vanilla pod and add them to the cream.
• Cook the custard over a gentle heat, stirring slowly all the time to prevent it from burning and curdling on the base of the pan.
• If the custard does overheat and so curdles, immediately strain it into a cold bowl and whisk vigorously to bring down the temperature. If it still looks curdled, blend in a food processor for a few seconds.
• Keep a close eye on the custards while baking as ovens vary so greatly (see Cook's tips on page 106).
• Work quickly when topping the custards, tilting the ramekins to form a thin, even layer of caramel before it cools and sets into a solid mass.

Cook's tips

• For best results, crème brûlée must be made with rich double cream and lightly baked until just set, no more. Traditionally, sugar is sprinkled in a thin layer over the surface of the custard and then flashed under a hot grill until it caramelizes. This is difficult to do well at home unless you have a very powerful grill. Under cooler heat, the sugar simply melts into burnt patches and the creamy custard starts to bubble through.
• Instead, make a caramel separately and pour this carefully over the custards to form a thin, even layer. Leave to chill in the refrigerator. After about one hour in the refrigerator, the surface seems slightly sticky but the caramel underneath remains quite crisp for several hours.

Orange and Cointreau Brûlée

SERVES 6

590 CALORIES/SERVING

2 oranges
568 ml (1 pint) carton double cream
6 egg yolks
40 g (1½ oz) caster sugar
45 ml (3 tbsp) Cointreau or Grand Marnier
75 g (3 oz) granulated sugar
pistachio nuts, to decorate

1 Pare the rind from the oranges. Add to the cream in a saucepan and bring slowly to just below the boil. Take off the heat, cover and infuse for 30 minutes.

2 Follow steps 2 and 3 of Crème Brûlée (see page 104), omitting the vanilla and straining the cream on to the egg yolks.

3 Pour the custard into a jug. Cool slightly, then stir in the Cointreau. Strain into a shallow ovenproof dish – we used a 21.5 cm (8½ inch) base measurement, 3 cm (1¼ inch) deep dish. Stand the dish in a roasting tin and pour in enough hand-hot water to come halfway up the sides.

4 Bake and chill as in step 5 of Crème Brûlée, cooking for 20–25 minutes only. (It will take less time than the ramekins as the custard is shallower.)

5 Finish with caramel as in step 6 of Crème Brûlée, preparing the caramel in one batch in a medium, heavy-based saucepan. Meanwhile, using a serrated knife, cut all peel and pith off the oranges and thinly slice. Cover and chill.

6 Top the brûlée with orange slices and pistachio nuts.

Cook's tips
• Ovens vary so greatly that cooking times can only be a rough guide. If you think your oven is hot, test the brûlées after 25 minutes, or if it's on the cool side, allow a few minutes longer.
• Vanilla pods are used for flavouring liquids such as milk, cream and sugar syrup. To give stronger flavour, add the vanilla seeds to the liquid (they're easy to scrape out of the warmed pods). The pods can be re-used if rinsed and dried after infusing.

Freezer notes
To freeze: Overwrap with freezer film and foil, and freeze at the end of step 4.
To use: Thaw at cool room temperature for 4 hours. Chill and complete.

Coconut Creams

Coconut cream powder can be found in some super-markets and most Chinese stores. It makes a very smooth custard, but if you can't find it, use 50 g (2 oz) block creamed coconut. The topping is a sauce, rather than a hard caramel.

SERVES 6

610 CALORIES/SERVING

50 g (2 oz) coconut cream powder or block creamed coconut, coarsely grated

568 ml (1 pint) carton double cream

6 egg yolks

40 g (1½ oz) caster sugar

75 g (3 oz) granulated sugar

1 large firm banana

toasted flaked coconut

1 Place the coconut cream powder or grated creamed coconut and the cream in a saucepan and bring slowly to just below the boil, whisking occasionally until almost smooth.

2 Follow steps 2, 3, 4 and 5 of Crème Brûlée (see page 104), omitting the vanilla. Make sure that all the coconut is rubbed through the sieve.

3 Place the granulated sugar in a small, heavy-based pan with 30 ml (2 tbsp) water. Heat gently until the sugar dissolves, then boil to a golden caramel. Take off the heat and immediately add 60 ml (4 tbsp) warm water (take care, as it will spit). Return to a gentle heat, stirring occasionally until smooth. Cool in a heatproof bowl.

4 Peel and thinly slice the banana, and stir into the sauce with a little flaked coconut. Spoon the sauce over the brûlées.

Freezer notes

To freeze: Overwrap and freeze at the end of step 2.
To use: Thaw at cool room temperature for 4 hours. Chill and complete.

Crème Caramel

SERVES 4–6

470–310 CALORIES/SERVING

175 g (6 oz) granulated sugar

1 vanilla pod or few drops of vanilla essence

568 ml (1 pint) milk

4 eggs

4 egg yolks

50–65 g (2–2½ oz) caster sugar, to taste

1 Slightly warm six ramekin dishes. To make the caramel, put the granulated sugar in a heavy-based saucepan over a low heat, and heat gently until it dissolves, brushing any sugar crystals down from the side of the pan to help it dissolve.

2 Bring to the boil and boil rapidly for a few minutes or until the syrup begins to turn pale brown, gently swirling the pan to ensure even browning. When the caramel is a rich golden brown colour, dip the base of the pan in cool water to prevent further cooking.

3 Pour a little caramel into each of the warmed ramekins and quickly rotate to coat the bottom and part way up the sides with caramel. Leave to cool.

4 To make the custard, split the vanilla pod to expose the seeds. Place in a pan with the milk and heat until almost boiling. If using vanilla essence, add after heating the milk. Meanwhile, beat together the eggs, egg yolks and caster sugar to taste until well mixed. Stir in the milk. Strain into a jug, then pour into the ramekins.

5 Place the ramekins in a roasting tin and pour in enough hand-hot water to come halfway up the sides of the dishes. Bake in the oven at 170°C (325°F) mark 3 for 20–30 minutes or until the custards are just set and a knife inserted in the centre comes out clean. Remove from the roasting tin and leave to cool.

6 To turn out, free the edges by pressing lightly with a fingertip, then run a knife around the edge of each custard. Place a serving dish over the top and invert. Lift off the ramekins. The caramel will have formed a sauce around the custard.

Syllabub

So many of our favourite pudding recipes are centuries old, and syllabub is no exception. It used to be made with warm milk taken straight from the cow and poured over sweetened wine, which gave it a frothy appearance. Sometimes spices were added or a spoonful of clotted cream floated on the top. Today's syllabub combines whipped cream, wine and lemon, and separates slightly as it stands.

Lemon Syllabub

SERVES 6

285 CALORIES/SERVING

finely grated rind and juice of 1 large lemon

150 ml (¼ pint) medium white wine

75 g (3 oz) caster sugar

284 ml (10 fl oz) carton double cream

2 egg whites

1 orange and 1 lime, to decorate

1 Put the lemon rind in a small bowl with 45 ml (3 tbsp) lemon juice, the wine and sugar. Leave to stand for about 15 minutes or until the sugar has dissolved, stirring occasionally.

2 In a medium-sized bowl, whip the cream until it holds its shape. Add about 60 ml (4 tbsp) of the wine mixture at a time, whisking well after each addition to ensure the cream thickens slightly again and will just hold its shape. It will splatter as you whisk so wear a large apron!

3 Whisk the egg whites until they stand in soft peaks. Using a large metal spoon, gently fold the egg whites into the wine mixture. Carefully spoon the syllabub into six tall glasses. Cover and refrigerate for at least 2 hours or overnight before serving. The longer the mixture is left to stand, the more it will separate.

4 Meanwhile, using a potato peeler, pare a little rind off the orange and lime. Scrape off any white pith, then cut the rind into very fine shreds. Blanch in boiling water for 1 minute, drain in a nylon sieve and rinse under cold running water. Dry on absorbent kitchen paper and sprinkle a little over each syllabub to serve.

Cook's tip
A sweet dessert wine would be delicious in this lemon syllabub, but as these can be expensive, we've made it with a medium white wine and added whisked egg white for extra lightness.

Watchpoints

- It's a good idea to scrub the lemon before grating it. Organic lemons have been found to be much juicier and fresher-tasting than ordinary lemons.
- Ensure the sugar has dissolved into the wine mixture before whisking it into the cream.
- Whisk the wine mixture into the cream slowly – if too much is added at once, the syllabub will become very thin and will quickly separate.
- Always use a dry, grease-free bowl when you are whisking egg whites.
- Whisk the egg whites until they are just stiff but not dry. If they are over-whipped, it is impossible to fold them evenly through the cream.
- Always cover syllabubs before putting them into the refrigerator or they will absorb flavours from other foods.

Strawberry and Lemon Syllabub Trifle (page 110)

Strawberry and Lemon Syllabub Trifle

This light pudding makes a refreshing change from the traditional rich trifle. Don't let it stand for too long after preparation – juices will leach out of the strawberries and the syllabub will separate.

SERVES 6

250 CALORIES/SERVING

450 g (1 lb) strawberries, hulled and quartered
125 g (4 oz) ratafia biscuits
75 ml (3 fl oz) sweet white wine
75 g (3 oz) caster sugar
30 ml (2 tbsp) brandy
finely grated rind and juice of 1 lemon
142 ml (5 fl oz) carton double cream
2 egg whites
rose petals, to decorate (optional)

1 Mix the strawberries with the biscuits, reserving a few of each for decoration if wished. Pile into a deep glass bowl and pour 30 ml (2 tbsp) of the wine over.
2 Mix together the remaining wine, sugar and brandy with the lemon rind and 45 ml (3 tbsp) lemon juice.
3 Whip the cream until just beginning to stiffen, then gradually whisk in the wine mixture.
4 Whisk the egg whites until stiff but not dry, and fold into the cream mixture. Pour over the strawberries and ratafias.
5 Cover and chill for no more than 2 hours before decorating with the remaining strawberries (plus biscuits and rose petals if wished).

Iced Port and Lemon Syllabub

SERVES 6–8

290–220 CALORIES/SERVING

1 large lemon
150 ml (¼ pint) port
50 g (2 oz) caster sugar
284 ml (10 fl oz) carton double cream
2 egg whites
frosted fruits or rose petals, to decorate (see below)

1 Follow steps 1 and 2 of Lemon Syllabub (see page 108), replacing the wine with port and reducing the amount of sugar as above.
2 Fold in the whisked egg whites as directed, then spoon the syllabub mixture into six or eight individual ramekin dishes or freezerproof glasses. Cover and freeze until firm, which will take at least 6 hours.
3 To serve, leave the syllabubs at cool room temperature for 10–15 minutes. Decorate with frosted fruits or rose petals and serve immediately.

Frosted fruits and rose petals
Choose firm, unblemished redcurrants, raspberries or grapes, or small, clean rose petals. Brush with some lightly beaten egg white and sprinkle with caster sugar. Place on non-stick baking parchment to set and leave in a cool place for no longer than 2 hours before using.

Old English Syllabub

SERVES 4

450 CALORIES/SERVING

1 clove
1 allspice berry
2.5 cm (1 inch) piece cinnamon stick
little freshly grated nutmeg
50 g (2 oz) caster sugar
finely grated rind and juice of 1 lemon
90 ml (6 tbsp) pale cream sherry
284 ml (10 fl oz) carton double cream
24 ratafia biscuits

1 Very finely grind the clove, allspice and cinnamon stick together with a pestle and mortar, then sift through a fine sieve.

2 Put the ground spices, nutmeg, sugar, lemon rind, lemon juice and sherry into a bowl. Stir well until the sugar dissolves, then cover and leave to stand for 1 hour.

3 Strain the sherry mixture through a fine nylon sieve into a clean bowl. Pour in the cream in a continuous stream, whisking all the time. Whip the cream mixture until it is just thick enough to hold a trail when the whisk is lifted.

4 Place four ratafias in each of four serving glasses, then cover with the syllabub. Chill for about 1 hour. Top with the remaining ratafias.

Sweet Soufflés

A cold, sweet soufflé looks impressive, and is surprisingly easy to make – just read the Watchpoints before you start. All sweet soufflés freeze well.

Lemon Soufflé

SERVES 6

480 CALORIES/SERVING

---

3 lemons

15 ml (1 level tbsp) powdered gelatine

4 eggs, size 2, separated

125 g (4 oz) caster sugar

450 ml (15 fl oz) double cream

finely grated rind of 2 lemons and 1 lime, to decorate

icing sugar, to dust

1 First prepare the soufflé dish. Cut a strip of double greaseproof paper long enough to fit around a 900 ml (1½ pint) soufflé dish and deep enough to stand about 7.5 cm (3 inches) above the top. Tie tightly with string so that the paper is held firmly around the dish and will not allow mixture to run out. Stand the soufflé dish on a plate.

2 Finely grate the rinds of the lemons and place in a deep bowl. Squeeze the juice from the lemons and strain 100 ml (4 fl oz) into a small heatproof bowl. Add 30 ml (2 tbsp) water and sprinkle over the gelatine. Leave to stand until the gelatine absorbs most of the liquid. Add the egg yolks and sugar to the lemon rind. With an electric whisk, beat until the mixture is thick, pale and mousse-like.

3 Dissolve the gelatine by standing the bowl over a pan of gently simmering water for about 5 minutes or until the gelatine clears and liquefies. Make sure that all the grains have dissolved. Don't be tempted to allow the water under the gelatine to boil, as it will get too hot and lose its setting quality.

4 Pour the warm gelatine quickly on to the egg yolk mixture, gently whisking to make sure it is evenly distributed. Lightly whip 300 ml (10 fl oz) cream until it just holds its shape – it should be the same consistency as the mousse mixture. Gently fold the cream into the mousse mixture with a large metal spoon.

5 Stand the bowl in a larger bowl filled with iced water. Stir the mixture from time to time until it is on the point of setting. Remove from the iced water immediately. Whisk the egg whites until they flop over in very soft peaks. Stir one large spoonful into the egg yolk mixture, then gently fold in the remaining egg white. Pour slowly into the prepared dish and shake gently to level the surface. Cover and refrigerate for about 3 hours or until set.

6 Carefully ease the paper away from the sides of the soufflé, holding a palette knife against the paper to stop the soufflé 'tearing'. Whip the remaining cream until it just holds its shape, and spoon it into a piping bag fitted with a 1 cm (½ inch) star nozzle. Use to decorate the top of the soufflé. Press the lemon and lime rinds into the soufflé edge. Refrigerate until required. Dust with icing sugar just before serving.

Freezer notes

To freeze: Prepare to the end of step 6, remove the paper and open freeze. Overwrap once firm.
To use: Thaw overnight in the refrigerator and finish as in the recipe.

Watchpoints

- Separate the eggs carefully; egg white that has traces of egg yolk in it won't whisk.
- Finely grate the lemon rind – coarse rind can be unpleasant.
- Lightly whip the cream until it just holds its shape.
- Whip egg white until it forms soft peaks so that it can be mixed evenly into the soufflé. The trick is to get all the mixtures, i.e. egg and sugar, cream, and egg white, to similar consistencies so that they fold together quickly and evenly.
- Dissolve the soaked gelatine very gently. Don't allow the water to boil furiously underneath – if gelatine gets too hot and boils it will not set.
- At step 5, if the mixture sets before the egg white is added, don't panic. Stand the bowl over a pan of gently simmering water until the warmth is sufficient to melt the mixture again. Stir frequently and don't let the mixture get too hot, then cool again and complete as directed. The soufflé won't be quite as light and airy as it could be, but it will be perfectly acceptable.
- After pouring the mixture into the prepared dish, do not attempt to level the surface with a spoon or spatula as you will lose all the air in the mixture and end up with a flatter, denser soufflé.

Raw eggs

The young, the elderly, pregnant women and people with immune-deficiency diseases should not eat raw eggs due to the possible salmonella risk.

Orange and Praline Soufflés

You can make the praline for these soufflés two or three days in advance and store it in an airtight container. This soufflé is actually more like an ice cream – freeze any left over for another day.

MAKES ABOUT 12 SOUFFLÉS

300 CALORIES/SERVING

50 g (2 oz) almonds with skins

125 g (4 oz) caster sugar

1 lemon

2 thin-skinned oranges

15 ml (1 level tbsp) powdered gelatine

4 eggs, size 2, separated

300 ml (10 fl oz) carton double cream

whipped cream, extra praline and caramelized almonds (see below), to decorate

1 Place the almonds and 50 g (2 oz) sugar in a small, heavy-based saucepan. Heat gently until the sugar melts and caramelizes. Do not stir; simply prod the sugar occasionally to help it melt evenly. Immediately pour out on to an oiled baking sheet and cool. Once cold, grind to a powder in a food processor or nut mouli.

2 Follow steps 2–5 of Lemon Soufflé (see page 112), using the finely grated rind of 1 lemon and 2 oranges in place of the 3 lemons, and 45 ml (3 tbsp) lemon juice with 100 ml (4 fl oz) orange juice in place of the 100 ml (4 fl oz) lemon juice. Whisk the egg yolks with only 50 g (2 oz) sugar. Add the liquefied gelatine and cream as directed, and fold the praline into the soufflé mixture with the whisked egg white.

3 Divide between about twelve 150 ml (¼ pint) ramekin dishes, levelling the surface. Freeze for about 5 hours or until firm.

4 To serve, leave at room temperature for 10–15 minutes and decorate with cream, praline and caramelized almonds.

Caramelized almonds
Follow step 1 of Orange and Praline Soufflé, using flaked almonds. Spoon about 12 uneven spoonfuls on to the baking sheet and cool. Ease off the baking sheet and store in an airtight container for up to 24 hours.

Double Chocolate Soufflé

This rich soufflé makes a really luscious dessert. To serve, cut it into wedge-shaped portions using a warm knife.

SERVES 8

690 CALORIES/SERVING

two 200 g (7 oz) bars plain chocolate

200 ml (7 fl oz) double cream

30 ml (2 tbsp) Cointreau or Grand Marnier

10 ml (2 level tsp) powdered gelatine

3 eggs, size 2, separated

50 g (2 oz) caster sugar

white, milk and plain chocolate curls (see page 115), to decorate

cocoa powder, to dust

1 Lightly grease a 21.5 cm (8½ inch) moule à manqué tin (see page 132) and line the base and sides with non-stick baking parchment, keeping the sides as smooth as possible. Stand the mould on a baking sheet.

2 Break up one bar of chocolate and place it in a small heatproof bowl. Melt slowly over a saucepan of simmering water, stirring gently until the chocolate is smooth. Leave to cool slightly.

3 Spoon the chocolate into the centre of the mould. Gently tip and brush it up the sides of the mould to coat the base and sides of the tin evenly (a pastry brush will help). Freeze for about 1 hour or until firm. Carefully ease off the tin and gently peel away the non-stick baking parchment. Place the chocolate case on a baking sheet in the refrigerator.

4 To prepare the soufflé, break up the remaining bar of plain chocolate and place it in a small heatproof bowl with 45 ml (3 tbsp) cream and the Cointreau. Melt over a pan of simmering water, stirring gently until smooth. Leave the mixture to cool slightly.

5 Soak and dissolve the gelatine in 30 ml (2 tbsp) water as in steps 2 and 3 of Lemon Soufflé (see page 112). Whisk the egg yolks with the sugar until the mixture becomes thick and mousse-like. Next, stir in the dissolved gelatine and the cooled chocolate mixture. Lightly whip the remaining cream, and fold it into the mixture.

6 Whisk the egg white until it forms soft peaks and fold it into the chocolate mixture. Pour gently into the

chocolate case. Refrigerate for about 3 hours or until set.
7 To complete, top with chocolate curls or shavings of white chocolate and leave at room temperature for 10–15 minutes before serving, to soften slightly. Dust with cocoa powder to serve.

Chocolate curls

Melt 125 g (4 oz) each of white, milk and plain chocolate separately as in step 2 of Double Chocolate Soufflé, stirring occasionally. Cover two rolling pins with non-stick baking parchment, secured with tape. Sit them on a wire rack over a baking sheet. When the chocolate has melted, use a teaspoon or fork to drizzle the chocolate back and forth over the rolling pins. Chill until set. Gently ease the chocolate off the parchment to produce 'curls', and return them to the refrigerator or freezer until ready to use. If you're skilled with a greaseproof paper piping bag, you'll find it easier to pipe the melted chocolate over the rolling pins.

Peach and Passion Fruit Soufflé

If you don't have a straight-sided soufflé dish, use a large 2.8 litre (5 pint) glass serving bowl instead, omitting the greaseproof collar.

SERVES 8–10

315-250 CALORIES/SERVING

| 450 g (1 lb) small ripe peaches |
| 1 large ripe mango |
| 3 large passion fruit |
| 50 ml (2 fl oz) orange juice |
| powdered gelatine |
| 4 eggs, size 2, separated |
| 125 g (4 oz) caster sugar |
| 284 ml (10 fl oz) carton double cream |

1 Tie a double band of greaseproof paper round a 1.7 litre (3 pint) straight-sided soufflé dish to stand about 5 cm (2 inches) above the rim, as described in step 1 of Lemon Soufflé (see page 112).

2 Wash, halve and stone all but one of the peaches. Roughly chop the flesh. Peel the mango and slice the flesh off the stone. Place the peach and mango flesh in a large saucepan with the pulp of one passion fruit and the orange juice. Heat gently, stirring continuously for 3–4 minutes or until soft and pulpy. Purée in a blender or food processor and rub through a nylon sieve. There should be 450–600 ml (¾–1 pint) purée.
3 In a small heatproof bowl, sprinkle 30 ml (2 level tbsp) powdered gelatine over 90 ml (6 tbsp) water and leave to soak for 5 minutes.
4 Whisk together the egg yolks and sugar until thick, mousse-like and pale. Gradually whisk in the fruit purée.
5 Dissolve the gelatine over a saucepan of gently simmering water as described in step 3 of Lemon Soufflé.
6 Following steps 4 and 5 of Lemon Soufflé, whisk the gelatine into the mousse mixture, and fold in the whipped cream and whisked egg whites. Pour the mixture into the prepared soufflé dish and refrigerate for about 5 hours or until set.
7 Place the pulp of the two remaining passion fruit in a small bowl with 150 ml (¼ pint) water. Sprinkle over 7.5 ml (1½ tsp) powdered gelatine. Leave to soak for about 5 minutes, then heat gently to dissolve, as described in step 3 of Lemon Soufflé. Cool the passion fruit gelatine mixture until beginning to set.
8 Thinly slice the remaining peach and arrange at random over the surface of the soufflé. Spoon the passion fruit gelatine mixture over the peach slices. Refrigerate for about 1 hour or until set. Carefully peel away the greaseproof paper collar as described in step 6 of Lemon Soufflé.

Cook's tip

Passion fruit (also known as granadilla and grenadilla) is a tropical vine fruit that usually looks like a large wrinkled purple plum. Passion fruit originated in South America but are grown in the West Indies, Africa, Australia and Malaysia. The inedible skin of the passion fruit is deeply wrinkled when ripe, and the flesh is sweet and juicy and pitted with small edible black seeds. To eat raw, cut in half and scoop out the pulp with a spoon. Sieve the pulp to obtain the juice, and use to make drinks and sauces, or to flavour ice cream.

Steamed Sponge Puddings

Revive golden memories of nursery puddings with our up-dated, lighter version of steamed syrup sponge, which loses none of that old-fashioned flavour. The lemon and cardamom ensure the puddings are not too sweet, and steam-baking cuts cooking time considerably. The moulds are placed in a bain-marie of boiling water, then covered with foil and baked. This gives the benefits of steam without the problem of a damp kitchen.

Syrup Sponges

SERVES 6

450 CALORIES/SERVING

butter
2 lemons
180 ml (12 level tbsp) golden syrup
3 green cardamom pods
125 g (4 oz) caster sugar
2 eggs, beaten
125 g (4 oz) white self-raising flour
cream or custard, to accompany

1 Melt a little butter and brush it over the insides of six 150 ml (¼ pint) metal basins with a top diameter of 8 cm (3¼ inches). Base-line with non-stick parchment. Finely grate the rind of one lemon. Gently heat 15 ml (1 tbsp) lemon juice with 60 ml (4 tbsp) golden syrup until blended. Pour into the basins.

2 Split open the cardamom pods and extract the black seeds. Using a pestle and mortar, crush the seeds to a fine powder. Place in a bowl with the grated lemon rind and 125 g (4 oz) softened butter. Beat until the butter is soft – this is easiest with an electric whisk.

3 Gradually beat the sugar into the butter until the mixture is fluffy. Add the eggs, a little at a time, beating well. If the mixture shows signs of curdling, beat in a little flour. With a large metal spoon, lightly fold in the remaining flour with 15 ml (1 tbsp) lemon juice until just mixed.

4 Carefully spoon the sponge mixture on top of the syrup in the pudding basins, levelling the surfaces. Cut six pieces each of foil and non-stick baking parchment, about 18 cm (7 inches) square. Place each piece of foil on top of a parchment piece and make a pleat across the centre to allow for expansion. Brush the centre of the parchment with melted butter. Tie securely over the basins, parchment side down. Turn excess paper up.

5 Stand the basins in a roasting tin in which they just fit. Pour boiling water around them to come halfway up their sides. Cover the roasting tin with foil. Bake in the oven at 190°C (375°F) mark 5 for about 40 minutes. Uncover the roasting tin and gently press the top of one pudding. If cooked, it should be just firm to the touch. If it feels slightly soft, re-cover the roasting tin and bake for 5–10 minutes longer.

6 To make the sauce, pare the rind of the second lemon and shred. Blanch for 1 minute in boiling water, then drain. Heat gently with the remaining 120 ml (8 level tbsp) golden syrup and 30 ml (2 tbsp) lemon juice. Uncover the puddings, and loosen the edges with a blunt-edged knife. Turn on to plates, pouring over the sauce. Serve with cream or custard.

Steamed Fruit Pudding (page 118)

Cook's tip

These Syrup Sponges, and the Raisin and Vanilla Sponge Puddings and Sticky Toffee Puddings on pages 118 and 119, are made in small moulds, but all these recipes can be made in a 900 ml (1½ pint) basin, then steam-baked for about 1¼ hours (about 1 hour 40 minutes if frozen), if preferred.

Watchpoints

• To be sure the puddings do not stick, make sure the moulds are well greased and the butter is allowed to set before the sponge mixture is added.
• Beat the butter well so that it is really soft and light before adding the sugar and eggs. It will then combine more readily and the mixture is less likely to curdle.

• Add the eggs slowly, beating well after each addition, to ensure that they blend evenly with the creamed ingredients.
• If the sponge mixture begins to separate, beat in a little flour to stabilize it.
• For a really light sponge, gently fold in the remaining flour until just mixed. Over-stirring or beating at this stage will toughen the mixture.

• Ensure that the papers are securely tied on to the moulds so that water can't seep in while they're steaming.
• To enjoy the puddings at their best, serve immediately.

Raisin and Vanilla Sponge Puddings

These are smothered in delicious large raisins known as lexias or muscatels, which can be found in supermarkets or health-food stores. Each pudding serves two generously.

SERVES 4

570 CALORIES/SERVING

butter
75 g (3 oz) raisins, preferably large lexias
finely grated rind and juice of 1 lemon
50 g (2 oz) caster sugar
50 g (2 oz) soft light brown sugar
2 eggs, beaten
125 g (4 oz) white self-raising flour
5 ml (1 tsp) vanilla essence
custard, to accompany

1 Grease and base-line two 300 ml (½ pint) pudding basins as in step 1 of Syrup Sponges (see page 116). Refrigerate to set the butter. Press the raisins all over the insides of the basins.

2 Follow steps 2 and 3 of Syrup Sponges, omitting the cardamom and folding in the vanilla essence with the self-raising flour. Spoon the mixture carefully into the prepared pudding basins.

3 Complete as in steps 4 and 5 of Syrup Sponges, baking the puddings for about 50 minutes.

4 Using a blunt-edge knife, gently ease the puddings away from the sides of the basins, taking great care not to disturb the raisins. Turn out and serve immediately, accompanied by custard.

Steamed Fruit Pudding

SERVES 4

580 CALORIES/SERVING

450 g (1 lb) fruit, prepared and stewed, or drained canned fruit
125 g (4 oz) butter or margarine
125 g (4 oz) caster sugar
few drops of vanilla essence
2 eggs, beaten
175 g (6 oz) white self-raising flour
a little milk, to mix

1 Half fill a steamer or large saucepan with water and put it on to boil. Grease a 900 ml (1½ pint) pudding basin and spoon the fruit into the bottom.

2 Cream the butter and sugar together in a bowl until pale and fluffy. Stir in the vanilla essence. Add the eggs and flour as described in step 3 of Syrup Sponges (see page 116), adding a little milk instead of the lemon juice to give a dropping consistency. Spoon the mixture into the prepared pudding basin.

3 Cut squares of non-stick parchment and foil large enough to cover the top of the basin, and secure over the basin as described in step 4 of Syrup Sponges. Place in the steamer or large saucepan of water, and steam for 1½ hours.

4 Run a blunt-edged knife around the top of the sponge and turn out on to a serving plate. Serve with custard.

VARIATIONS

For all of these variations, omit the stewed fruit.

Suet Pudding
Put 30 ml (2 level tbsp) jam in the bottom of the basin. Mix together 175 g (6 oz) self-raising flour, a pinch of salt, 75 g (3 oz) shredded suet, 50 g (2 oz) caster sugar and 150 ml (¼ pint) milk. Cook as above for 1½–2 hours.

Syrup or Jam Pudding
Put 30 ml (2 tbsp) golden syrup or jam into the bottom of the basin instead of the fruit.

Individual Dried Fruit Puddings
Add 75 g (3 oz) dried mixed fruit to the basic mixture. Spoon into greased dariole moulds and steam as for Steamed Castle Puddings (see below).

Mincemeat Puddings
Line the bottom and sides of the basin with a thin layer of mincemeat and fill with the sponge mixture. When the pudding is cooked, turn it out carefully so that the outside remains completely covered with the mincemeat.

Chocolate Pudding
Blend 60 ml (4 level tbsp) cocoa powder with 30 ml (2 tbsp) hot water, then gradually beat into the creamed mixture before adding the eggs.

Steamed Castle Puddings
Spoon a little jam in the bottom of greased dariole moulds and two-thirds fill with the sponge mixture. Cover each mould with greased foil and secure with string. Steam for 30–45 minutes (depending on size).

Sticky Toffee Puddings

To take the edge off the sweetness, we've added lemon juice to the topping for these sticky toffee puddings. Simply omit it if you prefer.

SERVES 6

540 CALORIES/SERVING

butter
125 g (4 oz) soft light brown sugar
60 ml (4 level tbsp) double cream
finely grated rind and juice of 1 lemon
50 g (2 oz) caster sugar
2 eggs, beaten
50 g (2 oz) pecan nuts, roughly chopped
125 g (4 oz) white self-raising flour
50 g (2 oz) toasted pecan nuts, to decorate
thin custard or single cream, to accompany

1 Grease and base-line six 100 ml (4 fl oz) dariole moulds as in step 1 of Syrup Sponges (see page 116).

2 To make the toffee sauce, place 50 g (2 oz) each of butter and soft light brown sugar in a saucepan with the cream and 15 ml (1 tbsp) lemon juice. Warm gently until blended. Pour half into the moulds.

3 Follow steps 2 and 3 of Syrup Sponges, omitting the cardamoms and beating the remaining brown sugar and the caster sugar with the butter. Fold in the chopped nuts with the flour and lemon juice. Spoon into the moulds.

4 Complete as in steps 4 and 5 of Syrup Sponges, cooking for 35 minutes.

5 Run a blunt-edged knife around each dariole mould and turn the puddings out on to individual serving plates. Decorate with toasted pecan nuts and the remaining warm toffee sauce. Serve with custard or cream.

Christmas Pudding

A deliciously rich pudding is a must for your festive table. Serve with Brandy Butter, some single cream or a thin custard flavoured with sherry and nutmeg.

Traditional Christmas Pudding

SERVES 10

445 CALORIES/SERVING

125 g (4 oz) butter
finely grated rind of 1 lemon
125 g (4 oz) soft dark brown sugar
2 eggs, beaten
50 g (2 oz) each blanched almonds (see Cook's tips), walnuts and Brazil nuts, roughly chopped
75 g (3 oz) carrots, coarsely grated
75 g (3 oz) pitted no-soak prunes, snipped into small pieces
350 g (12 oz) seedless raisins, currants and sultanas, mixed
25 g (1 oz) chopped mixed peel
50 g (2 oz) fresh brown breadcrumbs
125 g (4 oz) wholemeal plain flour
50 g (2 oz) white plain flour
15 ml (1 level tbsp) ground mixed spice
200 ml (7 fl oz) Guinness
30 ml (2 tbsp) brandy
30 ml (2 level tbsp) black treacle
brandy, to serve
about 10 silver coins, to serve (optional)
Brandy Butter (see page 123), to accompany

Freezer notes

To freeze: Freeze the pudding after 1 month's maturing.

To use: Thaw overnight at cool room temperature, then reheat as in step 4.

1 Beat the butter and finely grated lemon rind until soft. Gradually beat in the sugar, followed by the eggs. Mix in all the remaining ingredients, except the coins, brandy to serve and Brandy Butter, stirring well. Cover and leave in a cool place (not the refrigerator) overnight.

3 Steam the pudding for about 6 hours or stand the basin in a large saucepan filled with enough boiling water to come halfway up the sides of the basin. Cover and boil for about 4 hours. Cool the pudding completely, re-cover the basin with fresh greaseproof paper and foil, and refrigerate for up to 2 months.

2 The next day, lightly grease a 1.4–1.6 litre (2½–2¾ pint) pudding basin and base-line with non-stick baking parchment. Beat the pudding mixture again and spoon it into the basin. Pleat a piece of greased greaseproof paper and foil together, and then tie this securely over the pudding basin.

4 On the day, steam the pudding for about 3 hours or boil for about 2 hours. Turn out on to a warm serving plate. Warm about 60 ml (4 tbsp) brandy in a small saucepan, pour over the pudding and set alight. Baste with the flaming brandy, then serve, cut into wedges, with silver coins if wished, and accompanied by Brandy Butter.

Watchpoints

- Always leave the pudding mixture to stand overnight before you steam it, to allow the Guinness and brandy to plump up the dried fruits.
- Ensure that the paper is securely tied on to the pudding to prevent water seeping underneath it and into the basin.
- Always top up the pan with boiling water. The sudden drop in temperature caused by adding cold water can give a heavy pudding.
- If you're boiling the pudding, it's a good idea to stand the basin on a metal weight to lift it off the base of the saucepan. This stops the basin cracking.
- If you like a really dark pudding, steam it for 8 hours rather than 6 hours.
- We advise storing the pudding in the refrigerator; in warm, steamy places, such as the top of kitchen cupboards, puddings can go mouldy.

Cook's tips

- Blanched almonds are sold in supermarkets. To make them yourself, pour boiling water over the nuts, leave for 1–2 minutes, drain and pop out of their skins.
- We don't recommend adding coins or charms to the steaming pudding as they can taint the mixture when the pudding is left to mature. If you want to include coins, scrub them and slip them in as you serve each portion.

Iced Christmas Pudding

This unusual alternative to traditional Christmas pudding is made with raw egg yolks. The young, the elderly, pregnant women and people with immune-deficiency diseases should not eat raw eggs due to the possible risk of salmonella.

SERVES 8

454 CALORIES/SERVING

75 g (3 oz) no-soak dried apricots
75 g (3 oz) pitted no-soak prunes
225 g (8 oz) seedless raisins, currants and sultanas, mixed
100 ml (4 fl oz) brandy
450 ml (15 fl oz) double cream
4 egg yolks
60 ml (4 tbsp) golden syrup
mango and star fruit, to decorate

1 Snip the apricots and prunes into small pieces, and place in a bowl with the remaining fruit and brandy. Stir well, cover and leave in a cool place (not the refrigerator) overnight.

2 The next day, whip the cream until it just holds its shape. Whisk the egg yolks until thick and light in colour. Gently warm the syrup.

3 Mix all the ingredients together, cover and freeze for 2–3 hours or until beginning to firm up. Meanwhile, base-line a 1.1 litre (2 pint) pudding basin with non-stick baking parchment.

4 Stir the mixture to distribute the fruit through the cream. Spoon into the basin. Cover and freeze for 6–8 hours or until firm.

5 To serve, dip the basin into warm water. Loosen the edge of the pudding with a blunt-edged knife, then turn out. Serve in wedges or freeze until needed. Decorate with mango and star fruit slices.

Rich Figgy Pudding

Serve this pudding with a thin custard flavoured with nutmeg and sherry if wished.

SERVES 10

415 CALORIES/SERVING

125 g (4 oz) pitted no-soak prunes

250 g (9 oz) dried figs

125 g (4 oz) stoned dates

50 g (2 oz) walnuts, roughly chopped

125 g (4 oz) butter

finely grated rind and juice of 1 orange

125 g (4 oz) soft dark brown sugar

2 eggs, beaten

225 g (8 oz) cooking apples, peeled, cored and coarsely grated

50 g (2 oz) fresh brown breadcrumbs

125 g (4 oz) wholemeal plain flour

50 g (2 oz) white plain flour

15 ml (1 level tbsp) ground mixed spice

100 ml (4 fl oz) brandy

30 ml (2 tbsp) black treacle

toasted flaked almonds and icing sugar, to decorate

Nutmeg and Sherry Custard (see page 22), to accompany

1 Snip all the dried fruit into small pieces and mix together with the nuts.

2 Cream the butter with the orange rind. Gradually beat in the sugar, followed by the eggs. Add this mixture to the fruit and nuts with the apple, 75 ml (5 tbsp) strained orange juice and all the remaining ingredients. Beat well to mix. Cover and leave in a cool place (not the refrigerator) overnight.

3 Continue as in steps 2, 3 and 4 of Traditional Christmas Pudding (see page 121). Decorate with almonds and icing sugar.

Brandy Butter

SERVES 10

190 CALORIES/SERVING

125 g (4 oz) unsalted butter, softened

125 g (4 oz) icing sugar

25 g (1 oz) ground almonds

30 ml (2 tbsp) brandy

60 ml (4 tbsp) double cream

1 Cream the butter until very soft, then gradually beat in the icing sugar, ground almonds and brandy.

2 Gently stir in the double cream, cover and refrigerate.

3 Remove from the refrigerator at least 30 minutes before serving.

BAKING

This chapter features the mainstays of traditional cake-making – Creamed and Genoese sponges, fruit cakes and sweet yeast doughs used to make tea breads, hot cross buns and Chelsea Buns. The 'creaming' method of cake making is used for rich, buttery sponges, like Madeira, while light-as-air Genoese sponges are the best choice for fruit gâteaux to serve as dinner-party desserts.
The final section clearly illustrates how varied a Christmas cake can be. Traditionally, rich fruit cakes are baked months in advance of the festivities, but the alternative cake recipes given can be baked nearer the time. The Last-Minute Whisky Cake is best eaten freshly baked, while Golden Gifts, a unique recipe for making individual-sized Christmas cakes, need only be made a week in advance.

Tea Breads

The wonderful, sweet aroma of freshly baked tea bread is one of life's simple pleasures – and the taste is even better. For perfect bread, two things are essential: first, the dough must be really soft, and second, it must be well kneaded. All breads are best eaten on the day they're baked – especially when they're still warm from the oven.

Sweet Almond Bread

SERVES 10

325 CALORIES/SERVING

For the sweet bread dough

350 g (12 oz) white strong plain flour

5 ml (1 level tsp) salt

3.75 ml (¾ level tsp) ground mixed spice

butter or block margarine

finely grated rind of 1 lemon

7 g (¼ oz) sachet easy-blend dried yeast

25 g (1 oz) caster sugar

50 g (2 oz) currants

75 g (3 oz) raisins or sultanas

25 g (1 oz) cut mixed peel

40 g (1½ oz) flaked almonds

about 175 ml (6 fl oz) milk

1 egg, beaten

oil

To complete

melted butter

175 g (6 oz) almond paste

icing sugar, to dust

Freezer notes

To freeze: Pack and freeze before dusting with icing sugar.

To use: Leave wrapped and thaw overnight at cool room temperature. Wrap in foil and warm to serve.

1 Sift the flour, salt and spice into a bowl, and rub in 50 g (2 oz) butter. Mix in the lemon rind with the yeast, sugar, currants, raisins, mixed peel and almonds. Warm the milk until just hand hot. Make a well in the centre of the dry ingredients and add the milk and egg. Beat together to form a soft dough, adding a little more milk if necessary.

2 Turn out the dough on to a well floured surface and flour your hands. Start kneading the dough. Using the fingertips of one hand, bring the outsides of the dough into the centre and then, using the knuckles of the same hand, press the dough firmly away from you. Use the other hand to rotate the dough to ensure that it is evenly kneaded.

3 Continue kneading for 8–10 minutes or until the dough is elastic and almost smooth. Re-flour your hands and the work surface as necessary to prevent sticking. Place the dough in a large, lightly oiled bowl. Cover the bowl with oiled cling film or a floured tea towel and leave in a warm place for 1½–2 hours or until doubled in size.

4 Using floured hands, knock down the dough, then place on a lightly floured work surface and knead for 1–2 minutes only. Roll out the dough to a 25.5 cm (10 inch) square. Brush lightly with melted butter. Knead and roll out the almond paste to a strip about 23 × 10 cm (9 × 4 inches) and place down the centre of the dough. Fold the dough over the almond paste so that it just overlaps itself, sealing well.

5 Pinch the ends together to enclose the almond paste completely. Place the dough, seam side down, on a buttered baking sheet. Make a few shallow slits across the top with a sharp knife. (These should just mark the surface of the dough and not cut right through it.) Loosely cover with oiled cling film or a floured tea towel, and leave in a warm place to prove for 30–45 minutes or until doubled in size.

6 Uncover and bake in the oven at 190°C (375°F) mark 5 for about 40 minutes. When cooked, the dough should sound hollow when tapped. Cool on a wire rack. Dust with icing sugar.

Watchpoints

- The dough should be soft. If it is too dry, it will be difficult to knead and will not rise well.
- Thorough kneading is essential to give a light, even-textured tea bread.
- Any liquid added to the yeast should be tepid and the dough should be put in a warm, not hot, place to

rise. Excess heat retards the action of the yeast.
- Always cover the bowl when the dough is rising, to prevent a crust forming on the surface.
- Be flexible about timings for the rising and proving of the dough, which is greatly affected by the warmth of the day and the age of the yeast.

Cook's tip

We used quick-acting dried yeast, as it is readily available and simple to use. With this yeast the dough can be given just one rising: it's simply kneaded and then shaped straight away. But we found that a much lighter dough resulted from giving it the traditional two rises (this was especially true with the heavily

fruited doughs); 15 g (½ oz) fresh yeast or 7.5 ml (1½ level tsp) ordinary dried yeast could be used instead. First mix them with the warm milk, adding a little sugar to the dried yeast, and leave in a warm place for about 10 minutes before stirring into the flour.

Apricot and Pecan Ring

SERVES 10

335 CALORIES/SERVING

For the sweet bread dough

300 g (10 oz) no-soak dried apricots

125 g (4 oz) pecan nuts

350 g (12 oz) white strong plain flour

5 ml (1 level tsp) salt

3.75 ml (¾ level tsp) ground cinnamon

butter or block margarine

finely grated rind of 1 lemon

7 g (¼ oz) sachet easy-blend dried yeast

25 g (1 oz) caster sugar

about 175 ml (6 fl oz) milk

1 egg, beaten

oil

To complete

melted butter

about 120 ml (10 level tbsp) apricot jam

bay leaves

1 Snip 150 g (5 oz) apricots into small pieces; roughly chop 50 g (2 oz) pecan nuts. Follow steps 1–3 of Sweet Almond Bread (see page 126), omitting the spice, currants, raisins, peel and flaked almonds, and sifting the cinnamon with the flour. Stir in the snipped apricots and chopped nuts with the yeast.

2 Knock down the dough and knead lightly for 1–2 minutes. Roll out to an oblong measuring 61 × 15 cm (24 × 6 inches). Brush lightly with melted butter and fold into three lengthways (forming an oblong measuring 61 × 5 cm/24 × 2 inches). Roll gently to form a rope.

3 Place on a buttered baking sheet, seam side down, and shape into a ring, buttering and sealing the join well. Snip three-quarters of the way through the dough from the outer edge at 4 cm (1½ inch) intervals. Cover, prove and bake as in steps 5 and 6 of Sweet Almond Bread. Cool on a wire rack, then place on a flat serving platter.

4 Lightly grill the remaining pecan nuts. Boil the apricot jam with 15–30 ml (1–2 tbsp) water, sieve and cool slightly. Decorate the tea ring with the remaining apricots, pecan nuts and bay leaves, and brush with the apricot glaze.

Chelsea Buns

MAKES 12 BUNS

300 CALORIES/BUN

450 g (1 lb) white strong plain flour
5 ml (1 level tsp) salt
7 g (¼ oz) sachet easy-blend dried yeast
125 g (4 oz) butter
50 g (2 oz) caster sugar
1 egg, size 1, beaten
about 200 ml (7 fl oz) milk
3.75 ml (¾ level tsp) ground mixed spice
finely grated rind of 1 orange or lemon
50 g (2 oz) sultanas
50 g (2 oz) currants
50 g (2 oz) pistachios, almonds or hazelnuts, roughly chopped
For the glaze
50 g (2 oz) caster sugar
5 ml (1 tsp) orange flower water (optional)

1 Sift the flour and salt into a large bowl, and stir in the yeast. Rub in half the butter, then stir in half the sugar. Make a well in the centre. Stir the egg into the milk and pour into the well. Mix to a soft dough, adding a little more milk if necessary.

2 Turn the dough out on to a floured surface and knead well for about 5 minutes or until smooth and elastic. Place in a large oiled bowl. Cover with oiled cling film and leave to rise in a warm place for 1–2 hours or until doubled in size. Turn on to a floured surface, knead lightly, then roll out to a 30 cm (12 inch) square.

3 Cream the remaining butter with half the remaining sugar and dot over the dough, leaving a 2.5 cm (1 inch) border. Fold in half and roll out to the same size as before. Scatter the remaining ingredients over the dough, leaving a border, then roll up like a Swiss roll.

4 Cut the roll into 12 slices. Arrange the slices, cut side up, in a greased 23 × 28 cm (8 × 11 inch) baking tin. Cover and leave in a warm place for 15–20 minutes or until the pieces are doubled in size.

5 Bake in the oven at 200°C (400°F) mark 6 for 25–30 minutes. Transfer to a wire rack. For the glaze, dissolve the sugar in 75 ml (3 fl oz) water over a low heat, then boil for 2–3 minutes until syrupy. Stir in the orange flower water, if using. Brush over the warm buns.

Mini Hot Cross Buns

These buns are mildly spiced. If you prefer a stronger flavour, add another 2.5 ml (½ level tsp) ground mixed spice.

MAKES ABOUT 25 BUNS

95 CALORIES/BUN

For the sweet bread dough
350 g (12 oz) white strong plain flour
5 ml (1 level tsp) salt
5 ml (1 level tsp) ground mixed spice
5 ml (1 level tsp) ground cinnamon
5 ml (1 level tsp) freshly grated nutmeg
butter or block margarine
finely grated rind of 1 lemon
7 g (¼ oz) sachet easy-blend dried yeast
25 g (1 oz) caster sugar
75 g (3 oz) currants
25 g (1 oz) cut mixed peel
about 175 ml (6 fl oz) milk
1 egg, beaten
oil
To complete
75 g (3 oz) ready-made shortcrust pastry
beaten egg, to glaze
butter, to serve (optional)

1 Follow steps 1–3 of Sweet Almond Bread (see page 126), omitting the raisins and flaked almonds, and sifting the extra spices with the flour.

2 Knock down the dough and knead lightly for 1–2 minutes. Divide the dough into equal-sized pieces, about 25 g (1 oz) each, and knead each one into a small ball. Place on buttered baking sheets, seam side down, and flatten slightly with the heel of your hand.

3 Roll out the pastry and cut into narrow strips about 4 cm × 5 mm (1½ × ¼ inch). Glaze the buns with beaten egg and top with a pastry cross. Glaze again.

4 Leave the buns, uncovered, in a warm place for about 30 minutes or until doubled in size.

5 Bake in the oven at 190°C (375°F) mark 5 for 15–18 minutes or until they are well browned and sound hollow when tapped. Cool on wire racks. Serve lightly buttered if wished.

Creamed Sponge Cakes

Butter-rich and moist, sponge cakes made by the creaming method are always popular. The fat and sugar are 'creamed' together until as pale and fluffy as whipped cream, the eggs are beaten in, and the flour is then folded in.

Victoria Sandwich Cake

MAKES 8 SLICES

370 CALORIES/SLICE

175 g (6 oz) butter or margarine, softened

175 g (6 oz) caster sugar

3 eggs, size 3, beaten

175 g (6 oz) white self-raising flour

To finish

45–60 ml (3–4 level tbsp) jam

caster sugar, for dredging

1 Grease and base-line two 18 cm (7 inch) sandwich tins. Cream the butter and sugar together until pale and fluffy.

3 Fold in half the flour, using a large metal spoon, then fold in the remainder.

5 Turn out and leave to cool on a wire rack. When the cakes are cool, sandwich them together with jam and dredge the top with sugar.

2 Add the eggs, a little at a time, beating well after each addition.

4 Divide the mixture evenly between the two prepared tins, and level the surface. Bake in the oven at 190°C (375°F) mark 5 for 20 minutes or until well risen, firm to the touch and beginning to shrink from the sides of the tins.

VARIATIONS

Chocolate
Replace 45 ml (3 level tbsp) flour with 45 ml (3 level tbsp) cocoa powder. Sandwich the cakes with Chocolate Butter Cream (see page 133).

Coffee
Add 10 ml (2 level tsp) instant coffee powder, dissolved in a little warm water, to the creamed butter and sugar mixture with the eggs, or use 10 ml (2 tsp) coffee essence. Sandwich the cakes with Coffee Butter Cream (see page 133).

Orange or Lemon
Add the finely grated rind of an orange or lemon to the mixture. Sandwich the cakes with Orange or Lemon Butter Cream (see page 133).

All-in-One Cake
Add 5 ml (1 level tsp) baking powder to the basic recipe. Simply put all the ingredients in a large bowl or food processor and beat until smooth and glossy.

Freezer notes
To freeze: Wrap and freeze sponges after baking and cooling.
To use: Leave wrapped and thaw at cool room temperature for about 2 hours. Fill and decorate as required.

Watchpoints

• You need a mixing bowl large enough to accommodate vigorous beating without any danger of the ingredients overflowing.
• If beating by hand, use a wooden spoon and warm the bowl first to make the creaming process easier.
• Scrape the mixture down from the sides of the bowl from time to time to ensure no sugar crystals are left.
• An electric mixer is a time and labour-saving alternative to creaming by hand, but remember it cannot be used for incorporating the flour.
• Use eggs at room temperature and beat thoroughly after each addition to reduce the risk of the mixture curdling. (A mixture that curdles holds less air and produces a heavy, dense cake.) As an extra precaution against the mixture curdling, add a spoonful of the sifted flour with the second and every following addition of egg, and beat thoroughly. To keep the mixture light, fold in the remaining flour gradually, using a large metal spoon.
• For even cooking, bake both cakes on the same shelf in the centre of the oven, staggering the tins on the shelf so they fit comfortably without touching each other or the oven walls.

Warm Lemon Syrup Cake

MAKES 12 SLICES

360 CALORIES/SLICE

225 g (8 oz) butter or margarine, softened

finely grated rind of 2 lemons

225 g (8 oz) caster sugar

4 eggs, size 2, beaten

225 g (8 oz) white self-raising flour

65 g (2½ oz) candied lemon peel, finely chopped (optional)

30 ml (2 tbsp) lemon juice

For the syrup

175 g (6 oz) caster sugar

juice of 3 lemons, strained

1 Grease and base-line a 22 cm (8½ inch) base measurement moule à manqué tin (see note).
2 Cream the butter and lemon rind together in a bowl. Gradually beat in the caster sugar, followed by the eggs. Fold in the flour, candied peel and lemon juice.
3 Spoon the mixture into the prepared tin and level the surface. Bake in the oven at 180°C (350°F) mark 4 for about 1 hour or until well browned.
4 Meanwhile, prepare the syrup. Place the sugar, lemon juice and 75 ml (3 fl oz) water in a saucepan. Heat gently until the sugar dissolves, then bring to the boil and bubble for 1 minute. Cool.

5 As soon as the cake is cooked, turn it out on to an edged dish and immediately spoon over the syrup. Leave for about 30 minutes for the syrup to soak in. Serve warm, with lightly poached fruit if desired. Alternatively, cool completely and store in an airtight tin for up to 3–4 days.

Note
A moule à manqué tin is a deep cake tin with sloping sides; if unavailable, use a deep round cake tin of a similar diameter.

Madeira Cake

MAKES 12 SLICES

245 CALORIES/SLICE

125 g (4 oz) white plain flour

125 g (4 oz) white self-raising flour

175 g (6 oz) butter or block margarine, softened

175 g (6 oz) caster sugar

5 ml (1 tsp) vanilla essence

3 eggs, beaten

15–30 ml (1–2 tbsp) milk (optional)

2–3 thin slices citron peel

1 Grease and line a deep 18 cm (7 inch) round cake tin. Sift the plain and self-raising flours together.
2 Cream the butter and sugar together in a bowl until pale and fluffy, then beat in the vanilla essence. Add the eggs, a little at a time, beating well after each addition.
3 Fold in the sifted flours with a metal spoon, adding a little milk if necessary to give a dropping consistency.
4 Spoon the mixture into the prepared tin and level the surface. Bake in the oven at 180°C (350°F) mark 4 for 20 minutes. Lay the citron peel on top of the cake and bake for a further 40 minutes or until firm. Turn out and cool on a wire rack.

Rich Cherry Cake

12 SLICES

345 CALORIES/SLICE

225 g (8 oz) glacé cherries, halved
150 g (5 oz) white self-raising flour
50 g (2 oz) white plain flour
45 ml (3 level tbsp) cornflour
45 ml (3 level tbsp) ground almonds
175 g (6 oz) butter or block margarine, softened
175 g (6 oz) caster sugar
3 eggs, beaten
6 sugar cubes (optional)

1 Grease and base-line an 18 cm (7 inch) round cake tin. Wash the cherries and dry thoroughly. Sift the flours and cornflour together, and stir in the ground almonds and cherries.

2 Cream the butter and sugar together until pale and fluffy. Add the eggs, a little at a time, beating well after each addition. Fold in the dry ingredients.

3 Turn the mixture into the prepared tin, making sure the cherries are not grouped together, and hollow the centre slightly.

4 Roughly crush the sugar cubes with a rolling pin and scatter these over the cake, if liked.

5 Bake in the oven at 180°C (350°F) mark 4 for 1–1½ hours or until well risen and golden brown. Turn out and cool on a wire rack.

Butter Cream

MAKES 250 G (9 OZ)

125 CALORIES/25 G (1 OZ)

75 g (3 oz) butter, softened
175 g (6 oz) icing sugar
few drops of vanilla essence
15–30 ml (1–2 tbsp) milk or warm water

1 Cream the butter until very soft, and gradually sift and beat in the icing sugar.

2 Add a few drops of vanilla essence and enough milk or warm water to give a soft consistency.

VARIATIONS

Orange or Lemon
Replace the vanilla essence with a little finely grated orange or lemon rind. Add a little juice from the fruit, beating well to avoid curdling the mixture.

Walnut
Add 30 ml (2 level tbsp) finely chopped walnuts and mix well.

Almond
Add 30 ml (2 level tbsp) finely chopped toasted almonds and mix well.

Coffee
Replace the vanilla essence with 10 ml (2 level tsp) instant coffee powder blended with some of the liquid, or replace 15 ml (1 tbsp) of the liquid with the same amount of coffee essence.

Chocolate
Replace 15 ml (1 tbsp) of the liquid with 25–40 g (1–1½ oz) chocolate, melted, or dissolve 15 ml (1 level tbsp) cocoa powder in a little hot water and cool before adding to the mixture.

Mocha
Dissolve 5 ml (1 level tsp) cocoa powder and 10 ml (2 level tsp) instant coffee powder in a little warm water taken from the measured amount. Cool before adding to the mixture.

Genoese Sponge Cakes

Moist and light as air, a Genoese Sponge must be one of the most delicious cakes you can bake. Eggs and sugar are whisked until mousse-like, before flour is folded in with butter for added richness.

Genoese Sponge

SERVES 10

320 CALORIES/SERVING

For greasing the tin

white vegetable fat

caster sugar

flour

For the sponge

50 g (2 oz) unsalted butter

4 eggs, size 2

125 g (4 oz) caster sugar

90 g (3½ oz) white plain flour

caster sugar for dusting

To complete

90 ml (6 level tbsp) lemon curd

284 ml (10 fl oz) carton double or whipping cream, whipped

350 g (12 oz) fresh fruit such as blackberries, raspberries and sliced strawberries

icing sugar for dusting

Freezer notes
To freeze: Pack and freeze the cake after baking and cooling.
To use: Leave wrapped at cool room temperature for about 2 hours.

1 Brush a 21.5 cm (8½ inch) base measurement moule à manqué tin (see page 133) with melted white vegetable fat. Line the base with a disc of non-stick baking parchment and brush again with the melted fat. Once the fat has set, dust out the tin with caster sugar and flour.

2 Cut the butter into small cubes and place in a small heatproof bowl. Stand the bowl in a pan containing about 2.5 cm (1 inch) hot water, occasionally stirring the butter until it just melts. It should look creamy and opaque, not clear and oily. Immediately remove from the heat and cool slightly. Preheat the oven to 180°C (350°F) mark 4.

3 Place the eggs and sugar in a large deep bowl. With an electric mixer, whisk for about 10 minutes or until thick and mousse-like. The mixture should leave a trail in the bowl which remains visible for about 10 seconds. To speed up whisking, place the bowl over a pan of hot water, but don't let the eggs cook.

4 Sift half the flour over the surface of the egg mixture and carefully fold in, using a large metal spoon. Gently pour the liquid butter around the edge of the mixture, then sift over the remaining flour. Working very lightly, fold the butter and flour into the egg mixture until just incorporated. If you overwork the mixture, it will lose precious air. Gently pour the mixture into the tin and smooth over the surface.

5 Bake the cake in the oven for about 40 minutes. It should be well browned, have shrunk slightly away from the tin's side and should spring back when lightly pressed. Leave in the tin for 5 minutes, then run a blunt knife around the edge. Dust with caster sugar and top with baking parchment and a cooling rack. Holding tin and rack, turn both over. Shake the tin gently, then lift it off the cake. Peel off the lining paper and leave to cool. Carefully split into two layers with a large serrated knife.

6 To complete, slide a baking sheet between the halves and lift off the top. Place the base on a flat platter and spread with lemon curd. Top with lightly whipped cream and scatter over the fruit. Replace the top of the cake and dust with icing sugar.

Watchpoints

• Ensure that you fold in the butter very lightly; about 10 big sweeping folds with a basting spoon should be sufficient – a heavy hand will knock precious air out of the mixture. It's better to leave an occasional streak of butter or flour than to overdo the stirring, which will give the disappointing result of a flat, tough cake.

• The butter must be melted until pourable but still creamy – not oily – then folded into the mixture very lightly.
• To conserve as much air as possible, the sponge must be baked at once, so make sure the tin is prepared ahead and the oven heated and ready.
• The cake will be tight textured and dense if: the eggs and sugar are insufficiently

whisked at step 3, so that there is not enough air in the mixture; or the flour and butter are folded in too roughly, as this will knock out all air.
• The cake will not rise and will have a layer of butter on the bottom if: the butter is too hot and oily when added or is folded in too vigorously, causing it to sink through the mixture; or the ingredients are not correctly weighed so

you add too much butter.
• The cake will tend to sink in the centre if the oven door is opened before the cake mixture has had time to set.
• The cake will stick to the tin if: the tin is unevenly greased; or the tin is dusted with sugar and flour before the fat has set.

Ultimate Chocolate Cake

Perfect for a celebration, this is an excellent alternative to traditional iced cakes.

SERVES 10

620 CALORIES/SERVING

For the sponge

50 g (2 oz) unsalted butter
4 eggs, size 2
125 g (4 oz) caster sugar
90 g (3½ oz) white plain flour
15 ml (1 level tbsp) cocoa powder

For the mousse

125 g (4 oz) plain chocolate
5 ml (1 level tsp) powdered gelatine
50 g (2 oz) butter, softened
50 g (2 oz) caster sugar
2 eggs, size 2
15 ml (1 tbsp) Grand Marnier
142 ml (5 fl oz) carton double cream

To complete

275 g (10 oz) plain chocolate
100 ml (4 fl oz) double cream
mixed plain and milk chocolate leaves
125 g (4 oz) milk chocolate

1 Prepare a Chocolate Genoese Sponge as in steps 1–5 of Genoese Sponge (see page 134), sifting the cocoa with the flour. Cool the cake. Rinse and dry the moule à manqué tin. Line the base with a disc of non-stick baking parchment and the inside with a collar of paper, carefully stapling it together to form a straight edge. Place one of the sponge discs in the lined tin.

2 Melt the chocolate in a small heatproof bowl standing in a pan of hot water. Leave to cool. Using another small bowl, soak the gelatine in 15 ml (1 tbsp) cold water, then dissolve by standing in a pan of hot water.

3 Cream the butter, sugar and egg yolks until well blended. Beat in the cooled chocolate, Grand Marnier and gelatine. Stir in the lightly whipped cream and gently fold in the whisked egg whites to complete the mousse mixture.

4 Pour the mixture into the lined tin containing one disc of the sponge. Refrigerate for about 30 minutes or until beginning to set. Top with the second disc of Genoese Sponge and refrigerate for at least 3 hours or until set.

5 To complete the cake, remove from the tin and trim any excess mousse from the sides using a round-bladed knife. Place on a wire rack standing over a baking sheet. Break up 175 g (6 oz) plain chocolate and place in a bowl with the cream. Stand the bowl in a pan of simmering water until the chocolate melts, stirring occasionally. Don't overbeat. Cool until the mixture coats the back of the spoon. Pour over the cake, spreading it gently over the top and around the sides. Refrigerate to set.

6 To make the chocolate leaves, take a selection of clean, dry leaves (about 45–50 leaves will decorate the cake for a special occasion). Melt 125 g (4 oz) each of the remaining plain and milk chocolate in separate bowls and brush over the backs of the leaves. Take care not to let chocolate run over the edges of the leaves, or once set it will be difficult to peel off the leaves. Freeze to set. Repeat the coating until the leaves are covered with an even layer of chocolate. Once set, peel off the leaves.

7 To serve, place the cake on a flat platter and leave at room temperature for about 30 minutes before serving topped with chocolate leaves.

Mango and Cardamom Gâteau

Serve this delicious sponge as a dinner party dessert or for a special occasion tea. The mix of cardamom seeds and saffron strands adds a subtle fragrance to the sponge.

SERVES 10

330 CALORIES/SERVING

For the sponge

4 green cardamom pods

good pinch of saffron strands

50 g (2 oz) unsalted butter

4 eggs, size 2

125 g (4 oz) caster sugar

90 g (3½ oz) white plain flour

To complete

142 ml (5 fl oz) carton double cream

141 g (5 oz) carton Greek natural yogurt

icing sugar

2 large ripe mangoes

60 ml (4 tbsp) orange juice

crystallized orange slices, to decorate

1 Split the cardamom pods and remove the black seeds. Crush the seeds to a powder with the saffron strands. Prepare a Genoese Sponge as in steps 1–5 (see page 134), sifting the spices with the flour.

2 Whip the double cream until it holds its shape. Stir in the yogurt with 30 ml (2 level tbsp) icing sugar to make the cream mixture for the filling.

3 Sandwich the cake with the cream mixture and one sliced mango. Refrigerate for 2–3 hours, then dust with icing sugar and decorate with crystallized orange slices just before serving.

4 Meanwhile, liquidize the remaining mango flesh with 15 ml (1 level tbsp) icing sugar and the orange juice. Rub through a nylon sieve to remove all fibres. Cover and chill. Serve with the gâteau.

Red Fruit Gâteau

SERVES 10

490 CALORIES/SERVING

1 Genoese Sponge (see page 134)

450 g (1 lb) mixed summer fruit, prepared

300–450 ml (10–16 fl oz) double cream

frosted fruits and flowers (see page 110), to decorate

For the sauce

700 g (1½ lb) mixed red summer fruit, such as raspberries, strawberries, redcurrants and loganberries, prepared

sugar, to taste

45 ml (3 tbsp) lemon juice

1 To make the sauce, put the fruit, sugar and lemon juice into a saucepan and heat gently until the juice starts to run from the fruit and the sugar melts. Add 15–30 ml (1–2 tbsp) water and press through a nylon sieve, or purée and then sieve. Chill until ready to serve.

2 Cut the cake into two layers and sandwich together with some of the fruit sauce and the prepared fruit. Whip the cream until it holds its shape and spread it evenly over the top and sides of the cake. Decorate with frosted fruits and flowers. Serve the remaining sauce separately.

Christmas Cakes

There are several ways to guarantee success when it comes to making a rich, moist Christmas cake. One is to soak the fruit in brandy for a few hours before adding it to the cake mixture. Large, heavily fruited cakes improve with maturing, but if you've left it a bit late, try one of our variations, which are best served fresh with little or no maturing needed.

Jewelled Christmas Cake

SERVES 20

340 CALORIES/SERVING

125 g (4 oz) glacé cherries

50 g (2 oz) no-soak dried apricots

225 g (8 oz) each currants, sultanas and seedless raisins

50 g (2 oz) chopped mixed peel

100 ml (4 fl oz) brandy

50 g (2 oz) blanched (skinned) almonds

50 g (2 oz) Brazil nuts

butter

finely grated rind of I lemon

225 g (8 oz) soft dark brown sugar

4 eggs, size 2

225 g (8 oz) white plain flour

5 ml (1 level tsp) ground mixed spice

2.5 ml (½ level tsp) ground cinnamon

1.25 ml (¼ level tsp) ground mace

30 ml (2 tbsp) milk

120 ml (8 level tbsp) apricot jam

selection of glacé fruit

1 Rinse the glacé cherries under cold running water to remove the syrup. Drain well, then dry completely on absorbent kitchen paper. Cut into quarters. Roughly chop the apricots. Place the cherries, apricots and the remaining dried fruit and peel in a bowl. Pour over 75 ml (3 fl oz) brandy, stirring well. Cover and leave to stand overnight. Roughly chop the almonds and Brazil nuts. Cover tightly and set aside.

2 Cut two circles of greaseproof paper to fit a 20.5 cm (8 inch) deep, round cake tin. Cut another sheet to go round the tin, three times its height. Fold in half and turn up a 2.5 cm (1 inch) cuff along the folded edge. Snip the rim every 2.5 cm (1 inch). Grease the tin, line with one disc of greaseproof paper, and fit the strip, snipped side down. Grease the paper in the base of the tin, and cover with the second disc.

3 Preferably using an electric whisk, beat 225 g (8 oz) butter with the lemon rind until soft and pale. Gradually beat in the sugar until blended. (Crush lumps out of the sugar before adding.) In a jug, lightly whisk the eggs, then slowly beat into the creamed ingredients. The mixture should have a smooth consistency after each addition of egg.

4 Sift together the flour, mixed spice, cinnamon and mace. Using a large metal spoon, gently fold the flour into the creamed ingredients along with the soaked fruit, nuts and milk. (Don't be tempted to beat the ingredients in at this stage or the cake mixture will become tough.) Spoon into the prepared cake tin and level the surface.

5 Tie a double band of brown paper around the outside of the tin. Place a double sheet of brown paper on the middle oven shelf and sit the cake tin on top. Bake in the oven at 150°C (300°F) mark 2 for about 3½ hours or until a skewer inserted in the centre comes out quite clean. (If necessary, cover lightly with foil to prevent overbrowning.) Leave to cool in the tin.

6 Skewer the surface and add the remaining brandy. Leave to soak in. Turn out, wrap in greaseproof paper and foil, and store for up to 3 months. To complete the cake, place it on a board and heat the jam with 15 ml (1 tbsp) water. Sieve and cool slightly, then brush the cake with glaze; top with glacé fruit and glaze again. Decorate with ribbon. Tent in foil and store in a cool place for up to a week.

Freezer notes

To freeze: Pack and freeze after maturing for about 2 weeks, but before glazing and adding the glacé fruit.
To use: Thaw overnight at cool room temperature, then complete as in step 6.

Watchpoints

• Crush out all lumps of sugar before use, or the cooked cake will have a pitted appearance where the sugar has melted.

• Add beaten eggs slowly or the cake mixture will curdle, resulting in a dry cake.

• Beat the butter, sugar and eggs until they're really light and fluffy – any curdling at this stage will result in a drier cake. Also, fold in the remaining ingredients gently; too much stirring at this stage toughens the cake and can make it rise unevenly.

• Always bake larger cakes at a low temperature – 150°C (300°F) mark 2 – but adjust the temperature according to your cooker's instructions. Too high a temperature can dry the cake out disastrously.

• Protect cakes from burning or drying on the outside by tying a double band of brown paper round the tin.

• Take all cooking times as a rough guide only, as ovens vary greatly. If you're using a fan-assisted oven, cooking times will be considerably shorter. Two-thirds of the way through the suggested cooking time, gently open the oven door to check the cake. If it appears cooked on the outside, you can test the centre with a fine skewer (see step 5).

• Large, heavily fruited cakes store well but small cakes or lightly fruited ones don't. Wrap large cakes well before storing in a cool, dry place.

• Don't despair if your cake seems a little dry. Pierce it with a fine skewer and 'feed it' with brandy, then wrap and store again.

Last-Minute Whisky Cake

This cake is so light that it's best eaten as fresh as possible. Either serve it within three days of making, or freeze ahead, and decorate at the last minute.

SERVES 16

690 CALORIES/SERVING

400 g (14 oz) sultanas

white vegetable fat for greasing

350 g (12 oz) white plain flour

175 g (6 oz) butter

175 g (6 oz) soft light brown sugar

3 eggs, beaten

3.75 ml (¾ level tsp) baking powder

whisky

45 ml (3 level tbsp) apricot jam

about 350 g (12 oz) white almond paste

500 g (1 lb 2 oz) packet all-in-one royal icing

fondant decorations (see below)

1 Cover the sultanas with cold water and soak overnight. Drain well and pat dry with absorbent kitchen paper. Grease and flour a 1.7 litre (3 pint) ring tin.

2 Beat the butter with the sugar until fluffy. Gradually beat in the eggs with a little flour. Fold in the sultanas and the remaining flour, sifted with the baking powder, and 75 ml (5 tbsp) whisky. Spoon the mixture into the tin.

3 Bake in the oven at 180°C (350°F) mark 4 for 1¼–1½ hours. When cooked, leave the cake to cool for about 5 minutes, then turn it out on to a wire rack to complete cooling. Pierce with a fine skewer and spoon over about 30 ml (2 tbsp) whisky.

4 Prepare the apricot glaze as in step 6 of Jewelled Christmas Cake (see page 138), and brush over the cake. Roll out some of the almond paste to a strip 5 × 20.5 cm (2 × 8 inches) and fit round the inner ring of the cake. Roll out the remaining almond paste to a 30.5 cm (12 inch) round and lift it over the ring. Carefully split the centre and mould the paste down into the inner ring and over the cake. Trim the base edge. Leave it to dry for about 6 hours or overnight.

5 Prepare the royal icing according to the packet instructions. Spoon the icing over the cake, and fork or spoon it up to achieve a rough effect. Surround with fondant decorations (see below), carefully pushing some into the top icing. Use cocktail sticks to prop the decorations up if necessary, keeping them hidden from view. Leave to dry at room temperature for about 2 hours.

Fondant decorations
Add a few drops of food colouring and a puff of peppermint denture fixative to ready-to-roll fondant icing (the fixative is safe to eat and hardens the fondant). Knead, then roll out to about 5 mm (¼ inch) thick and cut out shapes. Place on non-stick baking parchment and leave for 1–2 days to dry and harden. Christmas cutters can be bought from specialist kitchen shops or by mail order. Or, make templates by tracing shapes from Christmas cards.

Golden Gifts

To make these individual Christmas cakes we used small baked bean cans. Remove labels, rinse and dry well before use. The capacity is about 200 ml (7 fl oz) – any similar-sized cans would do.

MAKES 6 CAKES (EACH ONE SERVES 2)

700 CALORIES/HALF CAKE

half-quantity Jewelled Christmas Cake mixture (see page 138)

90 ml (6 level tbsp) apricot jam

two 250 g (8 oz) packets white almond paste

three 250 g (8 oz) packets fondant/ready-to-roll icing

paper stars, marzipan holly leaves and berries or ribbons, to finish

1 Follow step 1 of Jewelled Christmas Cake (see page 138), preparing half the quantity of mixture only. Use 45 ml (3 tbsp) only of brandy to soak the fruit.
2 Prepare six 227 g (8 oz) baked bean cans with greaseproof paper, as in step 2 of Jewelled Christmas Cake, turning up a rim of 1 cm (½ inch) only along the folded edge of the paper.
3 Prepare the cake mixture as in steps 3 and 4 of Jewelled Christmas Cake, dividing it among the cans. Tie brown paper around the tins and place on a baking sheet.
4 Bake the cakes in the oven at 170°C (325°F) mark 3 for 1–1¼ hours, then cool in the tins. Spoon over a little brandy, wrap and store for 1 week only.
5 Use a sharp knife to level the tops of the cakes, if necessary, and turn over, base side up. Heat the jam with 15 ml (1 tbsp) water, then sieve. While still warm, brush all over the cakes.
6 On a work surface dusted with icing sugar, roll out the almond paste quite thinly and cut out strips 23 cm (9 inches) long by 4.5 cm (1¾ inches) wide. Fit these around the cakes, then trim as necessary. Knead the almond paste trimmings, roll out and cut out six 7–7.5 cm (2¾–3 inch) discs. Fit these on top of the cakes. Roll gently over the top to neaten. Leave at room temperature for about 6 hours to dry out slightly.
7 Roll out the icing, one-sixth at a time, to a 16 cm (6½ inch) round. Lift over each cake and mould round the edges. Trim.
8 Top with a mass of paper stars or marzipan holly leaves and berries, or tie with ribbons.

White Christmas Cake

16–20 SLICES

595–476 CALORIES/SLICE

300 g (10 oz) mixed dried peaches, pears and apples, chopped

75 ml (5 tbsp) brandy

125 g (4 oz) no-soak dried apricots

125 g (4 oz) Brazil nuts

200 g (7 oz) butter or margarine, softened

200 g (7 oz) caster sugar

3 eggs, lightly beaten

225 g (8 oz) white plain flour

2.5 ml (½ level tsp) ground allspice

5 ml (1 tsp) vanilla essence

225 g (8 oz) candied citrus fruits, in pieces

To decorate

45 ml (3 tbsp) apricot jam, sieved

700 g (1½ lb) almond paste

2 egg whites

about 900 g (2 lb) icing sugar, sifted

gold and white ribbon and sugared almonds

1 Mix the chopped fruit with the brandy and leave to soak for 3 hours. Grease and line a 20 cm (8 inch) round deep cake tin.
2 Chop the apricots and Brazil nuts. Cream the butter and sugar until pale and fluffy. Gradually beat in the eggs, adding a little flour if the mixture begins to curdle.
3 Sift the remaining flour with the allspice and fold into the mixture with the vanilla. Fold in all the fruit and nuts, except the candied fruits. Spoon half the mixture into the prepared tin. Press the citrus fruit over the surface. Spread with the remaining mixture.
4 Bake in the centre of the oven at 140°C (275°F) mark 1 for 2 hours or until a skewer inserted into the centre comes out clean. Leave to cool in the tin for 1 hour.
5 Place the cake on a 25 cm (10 inch) cake board. Spread the top and sides with the jam. Roll out the almond paste and use to cover the cake. Trim off any excess paste around the base.
6 Lightly beat the egg whites in a large bowl, gradually beating in the icing sugar until the icing stands in soft peaks. Spread the icing over the cake until evenly covered. Lightly 'peak' the icing.
7 Decorate the top with ribbon and sugared almonds.

INDEX